THE
DEATH
OF
MR. GOODGAME

THE DEATH OF MR. GOODGAME
My Struggle to Get Sober

CHARLIE BINGHAM, JR.

THE DEATH OF MR.GOODGAME
Published by Purposely Created Publishing Group™
Copyright © 2020 Charlie Bingham, Jr.
All rights reserved.

No part of this book may be reproduced, distributed or transmitted in any form by any means, graphic, electronic, or mechanical, including photocopy, recording, taping, or by any information storage or retrieval system, without permission in writing from the publisher, except in the case of reprints in the context of reviews, quotes, or references.

Unless otherwise indicated, scripture quotations are from the Holy Bible, King James Version. All rights reserved.

Printed in the United States of America

ISBN: 978-1-64484-332-1

Special discounts are available on bulk quantity purchases by book clubs, associations and special interest groups. For details e-mail: charlie.bingham@gmail.com or call (888) 949-6228.

For information log on to
www.thedeathofmrgoodgame.com

TABLE OF CONTENTS

Foreword by Jaha Howard vii
Acknowledgments xi
Preface xiii
Introduction 1
Charlie Bingham Who? 3
Who Is Mr.GoodGame? 13
Chapter 1: A Message from God or Am I Tripping? 15
Chapter 2: The First Test 25
Chapter 3: Bro. Dashings and the Church 35
Chapter 4: Nia's Late and Haters Gone Hate 43
Chapter 5: Nia's Ultimatum and Herb's House 51
Chapter 6: Lala's Email 59
Chapter 7: Deuce Murdered 77
Chapter 8: Convo with Vick 87
Chapter 9: Pull of Sherman Merman's Coattail 97
Chapter 10: Back to the Ill Mill with Sheila 109
Chapter 11: See You at the Crossroads 117
Chapter 12: Emotional Confession—Mr.GoodGame Winning 129
Chapter 13: Sheila's Prayer for Us 137
Chapter 14: Talk with God 145

Chapter 15: A Month of Sobriety 151
Chapter 16: Mr.GoodGame Strikes—
 Loban's Tongue Ring Shorty 163
Chapter 17: Mr.GoodGame Strikes Again—
 Zoe and the Club 169
Chapter 18: Mr.GoodGame the Savage 181
Chapter 19: Apology to Nia and HIV
 Test Results 191
Chapter 20: Sherman Merman Again 201
Chapter 21: Mr.GoodGame Quickie After
 Church with Zoe 203
Chapter 22: Exposed? 209
Chapter 23: Email Exchange with Nia 225
Chapter 24: Final Response to Nia 233
Chapter 25: Sunshine Goes to Fight Night 239
Chapter 26: Mr.GoodGame Off the Ropes 249
Chapter 27: Drama, Drama, Drama, and
 an LSAT Score 255
Chapter 28: Too Close to Home 269
Chapter 29: Iceberg Slim's Pimp 275
Chapter 30: Talk with God 285
Chapter 31: Back in the Ill Mill 291
Chapter 32: Billy's Baptism and Big News 299
Chapter 33: Teaching Others How to Pray 301
Chapter 34: Mocha Returns 315
Epilogue 337
About the Author 341

FOREWORD

I know Charlie. I know the Charlie that attends church on Sundays and Wednesdays. I know the quick-witted family man with the infectious sense of humor. This man asks tough spiritual questions, not taking much at face value. He sacrifices for his church family and complete strangers with a warm heart—all this in an effort to let God use him to do good works.

I didn't know Mr.GoodGame. He is an egocentric figure that lurks in the background, giving hints of something murky behind the veil. He studies. He pounces. He gets what he wants. Mr. GoodGame is as selfish and cold as they come, a wolf among sheep.

But Charlie, that's my friend and partner in the faith. Together, we've been teaching the young adult Bible class at our church in Atlanta. We've carved out our unique style of presenting real-life Jesus with authenticity, practicality and transparency, calling the class the Homeboy Bible Commentary and Updates (HBCU). We feel strongly about being honest with God's word, especially when it conflicts with our religious traditions or culture. In an era when everything is filtered and Photoshopped, we'd like to think we take the mask off and keep the main thing the main thing: Real Jesus. He has a legal bend in his thinking. I have a medical and political bend in mine. When the Apostle Paul makes an argument for salvation in Jesus, we enjoy connecting the dots of the legal arguments, the political consequences and the spiritual health implications. It makes for a gospel message that comes to life for us and our students over the many years.

It's a passion for us that started around 2004 when we were both in professional school at Howard University. He was at the School of Law, and I was at the College of Dentistry. We were heavily involved in the college ministry with our small church family in Washington, DC. There was nowhere to hide in a smaller church, so attendance and ministry work were expected. At the time, I was a newbie in the faith. I didn't know Charlie's story, but I knew he had experienced some things. It made him relatable and that was different from most young church folks. It was comforting, especially since I had several bad habits that I was battling as a new Christian. But again, I knew Charlie, but I didn't know Mr.GoodGame . . . until now.

This book takes us behind the veil and gives us a raw inside view into spiritual warfare primarily between these different forces. The battle is a familiar one for those who are struggling to bend their will to God's will. We feel this narrow spiritual victory on one front all while losing badly on another front. This book shows us how we can have good intentions to minimize one character flaw while other flaws are raging like a wildfire with no end in sight.

We witness a faith walk that mimics one contradicting roller coaster after another. One minute, it exudes confidence and focus. The next moment, it's insecure and completely distracted. We see a heart to please God and a disregard of God's children in the same breath. We see a hyperfocus of particular sins and a willful ignorance of a host of other sins.

Not many books about one's Christian walk are going to be this exposed and honest. Most authors wouldn't dare print their paternalism, racism, misogyny, homophobia and traditionalism for full display. It's even more rare considering our mainstream society has become more sensitive to the unique experiences of marginalized groups.

As you read, be prepared to step in the mind of a young man who knows he needs God to live but is unsure if he wants to live for God. It will be uncomfortable and unsettling, but if we are honest, we can find some part of ourselves in his journey.

Jaha Howard

ACKNOWLEDGMENTS

Glory be to God!

To my wife, Babe, thanks for your faithfulness even when I was all over the place. Mom, thanks for planting so many righteous seeds in me to help me thrive in this world. You're the real MVP! Carlie and Charlie, thanks for giving me a reason to continue living and striving for excellence. For all those who are mentioned in this book, thanks for the lessons and please forgive me if I offended you. Life, thanks for the experiences. Milwaukee streets, thanks for putting the hustle in me and teaching me so many lessons. Daphne, Quala, Traci, Kelley, thanks so very much for the love and encouragement!

PREFACE

This book is for readers (Christian or not) who want to live a purpose-driven life but are struggling to find their purpose. In seeking to live with purpose, we often encounter a variety of obstacles. I know. I encountered several along my way, including wanting to do right but doing wrong, mental health issues, drug abuse, sexual promiscuity, generational curses, death, post-traumatic stress and others. I now feel like I'm living with purpose (even though I still struggle with some of these issues on a daily basis), and I hope publishing my truth on how I got here will help others struggling with the issues I've struggled with is a part of that. To overcome my issues, I started writing a journal in 2004 while a graduate student at Morgan State University, a historically black college and university (HBCU) located in Baltimore, Maryland.

    I decided that it was time to share my struggle to get sober as chronicled in my journal because my past is far behind me now. I learned from the mistakes I made during that time, and I'm no longer ashamed to share my ignorance during that period in my life as long as it will help others. My hope is that sharing my testimony will assist in someone else's deliverance. As I reread my journal in preparation for this book, I cringed at some of the entries based on my behavior, words and thoughts at the time and now realize that I was very chauvinistic.

Since I can remember, my mom always told me to keep a journal, but I didn't listen. You would've learned how I was an honor student on a full scholarship, but it also would've laid out a theme of a young man who, despite knowing God well, rebelled against His influence at almost every turn because he didn't think that God could use him.

I was a young churchgoing savage who was a whore, drug dealer and a part of a crime syndicate that resulted in Jackson State changing their book return policies. I was also a rapper. I was known around campus for my rapping skills, and during the end of my sophomore year, I received an invitation to go on tour and open up for Master P and Young Bleed. I knew from firsthand experience that the rap life would lead to a further life of sin. I was never a good rap writer, but my freestyles were bomb because I kept it real and talked about my life and what I had done. To fuel my freestyles, I essentially chose to use my God-given talents to live a savage life for my own glory and not God's.

I had a major decision to make, so I prayed hard and asked my mom to pray as well that I would make the right decision. I ended up making a pact with God that I would quit rapping if He would show me a way to use my talents for His glory. He did just that!

Looking back, it's clear to see that in spite of myself, God always protected me and pointed me in the right direction. I believe that is due in part to my mother. I've always told folks that I catch residual blessings because my mom is so consistently holy. She was a real-life example of someone trying to be Christ-like at every turn, including not divorcing a husband she knew to be a cheater as well as a verbally and physically abusive alcoholic. Perhaps this is why I was so chauvinistic—look at the example I had in a father. To add to this self-analysis, even though I was the third-born son, I was named after my father! However, that's no excuse because my mom did everything she could to make sure I was surrounded by good male role models growing up. I'm blessed to have my mom live with me today.

INTRODUCTION

What you are about to read is my real-life experience, my testimony and nothing but the raw truth. It's straight with no chaser! I've had to change some names for privacy reasons; other than that, it is the actual content I wrote all those years ago.

The book starts with a little bit more about me, where I'm from, significant life events that have impacted me, and why I ended up depressed when I started at Morgan State at 24 years old. I provide context where necessary, and in other places, I share my actual journal entries, which are written in an unfiltered stream of consciousness (that includes language I used back in 2004).

You will also be introduced to my alter ego at the time, Mr.GoodGame, who was responsible for me upholding generational curses, submitting to my fleshly desires and stumbling along the way.

Nonetheless, God preserved me through my struggles, so I try to glorify Him by my love, and the language for that love is action. I try to show His love to everyone I meet, and sharing this journey with you is me showing love. If you take nothing else from your read, please take with you that God loves you, you are fearfully and wonderfully made, and God can use you for His purposes despite your many flaws. I'm a living testament of this.

CHARLIE BINGHAM WHO?

I am a junior named after my father even though I am the third son and middle child of five. I had two older brothers who have since passed on—Victeur Bingham (Vick), the oldest, and Virgil Bingham (Tweety), who died when I was really young.[1] I also have two younger sisters—Charlene and Charity. I was born and raised on 27th and Chambers, one of the roughest neighborhoods in Milwaukee, Wisconsin. I spent significant time on 27th and 23rd and Chambers, which are located in the infamous 53206 zip code.

For context, Milwaukee is the most segregated city in America and is statistically the worst place for African-American males in the United States today.[2] The "deuces" where I grew up with my family is known as a crime-ridden neighborhood with gang violence, drugs and pervasive poverty.

---

1 Tweety died in 1984 at 10 years old from kidney failure when I was four years old. He was the poster child at the time for the National Kidney Foundation of Wisconsin and had two kidney transplants during his life. The second transplant he had bought him enough time to enjoy life as he got to see Micky Mouse at Disneyland and spend Thanksgiving and Christmas at home with his family. While living, Tweety brought joy to practically everyone he encountered due to his sunny disposition. Quoting Wisconsin Public Radio, "He looked at dying as being in heaven with God with no more needles, no more wheelchair, and being able to eat whatever he wanted."

2 https://www.wpr.org/report-milwaukee-racine-rank-worst-cities-african-americans-live

Back in the day, I described it as follows in one of my raps:

I was born in a jungle made of bricks
I had to be slick, straight sick
Had to stay sharp like schlick
Cause if you don't you might get yo wig split
Everybody in my hood got a purpose
Most you meet are very conversive
Trying to get that cheese cause in the Mill that's what we worship
It rules all pews, don't get it confused
Better catch the cues or end up on the evening news
Cause killers ain't amused, gotta pay your dues
Or you lose taking an L
The Mill home of choke artists like Sprewell
Pimps with pinky nails
Watch out for that catfishing
Pros on a mission
Peel-outs, pistols and burnouts we ditching
You know how we living – fast
In 6th gear like flash, bout that cash,
No one wants to end up last
Better stay on your Ps and Qs and that's for certain
Cause in the Mill, one slipup and it's curtains.

The Death of Mr.GoodGame

Coming up encouraged to have pros, nice clothes and game that easily flows
I suppose it's cause those who I admired were rappers, pimps, hustlers, drug dealers or killas for hire
It's odd cause without God
I'd probably be locked up somewhere like Oz
Pops was an alcoholic with game
Sweet talked a Christian girl and not too long after I came
Never really knew a male to be a real man,
From responsibility they all eventually ran
Now it's my turn and I'm trying to understand God's plan
Trying to be wise, patient, hardworking and humble
Go to work and pay Mom's bills and never mumble
Don't want to tumble and follow footsteps before me
Same routine 9 to 5 starting to bore me
Get home and a dirty house floors me
Maybe it's time to leave the nest
But mom is sick and needs her rest
This is the conflict I address
Week to week, month to month
Pressure mounts up, leading to blunt after blunt

Gotta learn to deal and cope
Sometimes I think I'd be better off selling dope
Gotta be the man that my pops wasn't
Taking care of a family and house got me bugging
Cause I ain't had one baby
But I feel like I got plenty and bout to go crazy

Living in this type of neighborhood created numerous obstacles and challenges. I consider myself blessed to have made it out and I'm constantly letting people know that I'm a survivor of Milwaukee by the grace of God. My mom was a community activist, and I was thought to be intelligent by our community based on her reputation. So even though I was involved in the street life, the drug dealers and gangsters gave me a pass. My mom always told us that knowledge is power, so for middle school, my mom bussed me and my sister to a Catholic school outside of the ghetto. My experience there was similar to the young lady in the movie *The Hate U Give*. I was forced to live a double life. Looking back, to be honest, as a matter of survival in two different worlds, I think this is where I began developing multiple personalities, and Mr.GoodGame was born.

As a result of the valuable education I received at that Catholic school, I was given a scholarship to one of the most prestigious Jesuit high schools in the state: Marquette University High School. At Marquette, I was required to take a theology class taught by a Jesuit priest. One day during class, I challenged the priest on a concept that was not based on biblical principles. My reputation at the school suffered as a consequence. The priest didn't know that I was very knowledgeable about the Bible and the origins of many Catholic traditions and rituals. I had an experience similar to the young man in the movie *Finding Forrester*. I received my first C, and my grades for the following semester weren't stellar either. I hated the experience so much that I begged my mother to put me in public school, and she finally relented.

At the public school, I ended up playing on the junior varsity basketball team that went on to be city champs. That year I started hanging with the wrong crowd—stealing cars, smoking weed, robbing folks with my older brother and doing other savage stuff. My mom abruptly moved us to a small town called Waynesboro, Mississippi, which was where my great-grandmother lived.

In Waynesboro, we lived without water for a year, so I was the musty kid at school. I also was ridiculed heavily for "talking proper" and was labeled a Yankee. Nonetheless, I excelled at school and was a point guard on the basketball team. At graduation I racked up on almost all of the academic awards and scholarships. I eventually went to a career fair where a smooth older African-American male told me that his school would pay for me to attend, and that is exactly what I did. I attended Jackson State on a full scholarship and even had extra scholarship money to live off. I majored in mass communications because I was a rapper at the time and knew that I could get in the on-campus studio as a mass communications major.

I sold weed my freshman year to everyone, including teachers and athletes. Unfortunately, due to my "24/7 open shop" mentality, my grades suffered and I lost half of my academic scholarship. After my freshman year, I stopped selling weed and focused on my academics. I was enrolled in the work study program and worked as a radio personality for the campus jazz station. After my sophomore year, I started getting 4.0s and changed my on-campus circle of associates. I kept my report cards in my wallet, which saved me from getting locked up by the cops for being in the wrong place at the wrong time twice back home in Milwaukee.

After graduation, I started working as a cameraman at a local news station and eventually transferred to a news station in Milwaukee. At the Milwaukee news station, I was a tape operator, which was a good-paying union position that prevented me from doing anything else at work during my shift. I quickly realized that I didn't need to go to college for four years to do my job, and my intellectual curiosity caused me to look for other opportunities to fulfill my purpose and have impact. Eventually I received an email about a Teach for America type of program in Baltimore. I moved to Baltimore and enrolled in a master of arts in teaching program at Morgan State University. There, I taught Advanced Drawing and Painting and Graphic Design at a local high school to juniors and seniors during the day and attended class at night. It was during this time period that I began my journal.

For more context, at Jackson State, I was "the man." I had great grades, was super popular, was loved by my professors, and had a great social life as far as relationships with the opposite sex were concerned. To give you a sense of how cocky I was, I actually refused to join a fraternity even though I was approached by a couple. I thought they would bring my social status down because I would have to associate with individuals I considered lame at the time. Why am I sharing this? Stay with me and you'll understand; details on my mindset really matter in this book.

After my freshman year, I went home and worked two jobs and saved up enough money to buy myself a Ford Explorer with cash and no help from anyone. I put some 15-inch speakers and a detachable CD face with a hidden CD changer in my truck. You couldn't tell me nothing when I got back on Jackson State's campus! Everyone knew my Ford Explorer, and my crew affectionately named it the "Purple Heater," which was very appropriate given that we smoked so much Purple Kush in the truck during that time.

My circle of friends was small because we were involved in activities meant to survive, and it was best that others never knew. While I knew practically everyone from selling weed and hanging out (and everyone knew of me), I say my circle was small because I really didn't allow too many to get close to me. My mom taught me at a young age that friends are far and few. I had a lot of associates, but very few I considered friends. One of the consequences of popularity is that people will gossip about you, but I never worried about that because only a few truly knew what I was about. One of the mottos that my crew established and tried to live by, based on a Young Bleed song, was to always come back better than we were the last time we left. Then, for the first time since we made the motto, I violated the principle—or so I thought—by driving a minivan to graduate school in Baltimore.

The summer before I was scheduled to drive to Baltimore, my mom drove my truck to work one Saturday morning against my wishes and got into a terrible accident that severed her leg. My truck was also badly damaged, and as a result, I had to drive my mom's minivan to Morgan State. That hurt my pride because I thought I was too good for a minivan. That played a big part in my downward spiral into a depression that led me to starting my journal.

WHO IS MR.GOODGAME?

Mr.GoodGame is my alter ego. I am a Gemini with a birthday of June 14th. As one of the constellations of the zodiac, the Gemini is symbolized by twins. We are said to have a dual personality with our strength lying in that versatility, and I definitely have the duality of twins. Mr.GoodGame would be the prideful, wild, selfish, emotionless, scheming, carefree twin that always seeks to please his flesh.

I've recently embraced the fact that I have about seven different personalities. One through three are loving, kind, concerned for others, helpful and well-mannered gentlemen. These personalities are a good reflection of the principles my mom instilled in me. Four and five are logical and act as my voice of reason. These two personalities are very balanced yet guarded to keep one through three from being taken advantage of. They developed out of necessity because in Milwaukee you have to be able to discern BS fairly quickly or you'll get eaten alive by the abundance of con men and women. Personalities six and seven are straight savages! They are heartless, selfish and impatient. They have no time for BS and can be straight wolves. Personalities six and seven are where Mr.GoodGame lives.

There are different levels of the characteristics described in one through three, four and five, and six and seven. For example, personality one is super loving, loyal, kind and concerned for others almost to a fault. Personality two is a little less extreme, and three is the least extreme as far as those characteristics go. Sometimes I am like Jesus to the extent of giving my last to others even if it hurts me, and other times I am more measured in how I give to others. These same levels apply to personalities four and five and six and seven. As you read you will see the distinction. Sometimes I'm harsh but not a savage; other times I am a straight savage.

I've wrestled with these different and conflicting personalities all of my life but didn't realize my changing moods until family and friends recently began pointing out my blind spots. The same way that people code-switch how they talk and otherwise behave to fit into a particular environment, I had to code-switch personalities to survive the many different worlds I found myself growing up in. You will see my battles with Mr.GoodGame and understand why I had to put him to death to succeed and get to my purpose-driven life.

1

A MESSAGE FROM GOD OR AM I TRIPPING?

9:00 a.m. Monday 7/26/04
Hello my name is Charlie Bingham and I want to invite you to walk and talk with me on my journey as I go through my struggle to get sober. This is day one and I'm sitting in the Morgan State University School of Graduate Studies typing on my computer. This is day one of a new beginning. From here on out, I will document the trials and tribulations that I endure along my way as I travel the road to recovery.

Last night I got high and stayed up until about three in the morning. When I finally got in the bed, I had the shakes cause I was high and began to think about how foolish it is for me to smoke and the reasons why I smoke. I am a true chronic smoker, and I probably smoke just as many Black and Milds as I do chronic. I have been smoking since I was 13 years old and I am well past the 10-year mark I set for myself to have fun and enjoy life, and I am still smoking. I come from a family filled with chronic smokers, mainly just weed and cigarettes, but keeping it real you know there are always a couple of hypes in every family. Anyway, more on those things later . . . that's just a brief background profile to help set the stage.

I am going to buy some journals and start writing at least once a day. I look at it as sort of therapy because everyone needs someone to talk to at one point or another. I know I definitely need someone to talk to because I have really been wilding. I am going to try to write four entries a day. I think that would be good enough to pretty much sum up my day and the experiences I have along the way. Last night the idea came to me while trying to go to sleep. I couldn't go to sleep because I was so high that the weed had me shaking uncontrollably. While thinking about why I smoke and trying to focus on how to stop the shaking and break the habit, out of nowhere a voice in my head spoke and said, "My son redeem the time before it's everlasting too late." I stopped shaking and began wondering about the voice because I knew what the message was and I have known for quite some time now.

I often look at myself sort of like Jonah in the Bible because I have felt the Spirit telling me to do this or that, and often I have ignored it or been too scared, or cowardly is a better word, to act. I have been very selfish and I most likely still am a very selfish person who just likes to have fun and do things my way. Well God let me do just that and since I've been in Baltimore I have really had no real joy. Anyway, I began to think about these things and every time my mind drifted to worldly matters I began to shake again. Eventually I fought the shakes off and began to have positive thoughts, and that's when a revelation hit me: Keep a journal and document your struggle to get sober.

I thought about it for a minute and thought about the consequences. Maybe when I do become sober, some young thug or struggling Christian may be able to read my struggle and be empowered in some way or another. When my thoughts began to drift away and my mind went back to my daily affairs, I would begin to shake again. It felt like God was sending me a message through my soul, but I was passing it off as me being high and my inner voice just talking to me. For a while I began to shake every time I let the ideas pass through my mind that it wasn't God. So here I am the next morning since I have no notebook typing my thoughts out. Yesterday morning I returned to church after about a three-month absence, even though I know better and was raised in the church. So this is my first entry on day one of my struggle to get sober.

Since these are my first entries I want to make sure that we have a proper introduction and that you know all the facts so that when things come up later you can truly *overstand*, not just understand, the situation. After writing the first entry, I decided to go to a Bible website to look at the scripture of the day.

Smoking is very foolish, yet I continue to do it. Some look at me and wonder how I can have so much knowledge and wisdom and continue to do something as foolish as smoking. Along the way I have become a slave to sin and especially smoking. Hopefully this will be my liberation from that lifestyle. Well this will be my liberation. One of my neighbors who I kick it with often told me yesterday that I was the dumbest smart guy that she knows, and quite frankly I would have to agree with her. I think I smoke to escape reality because to whom much is given much is expected and required, and I have been given much. I have knowledge that I keep to myself and probably could help a lot of people, but I am not always up to the task and so to fight and distort my consciousness I smoke and try to escape my responsibilities. Not anymore; it is really time to deal with life.

My mother raised me to be a preacher by constantly instilling in me the word, so I know that which is right. I just don't do it by choosing to do my own thing. I often find myself praying to God that He will have mercy on my soul. I pray that I can change and do His will before it's too late because I know I would have given up on a cat like me a long time ago. I have tried to stop smoking, and if you are a smoker you know what I am talking about, probably well over 100 times in my 11-year span.

Because I'm not too foolish, I know that I absolutely cannot and should not embark upon this journey without God, so I went to the Bible website to get a verse to think about so that I can reflect back to that and keep the evil thoughts out my head. Thoughts about my past and my sinful relationships. I came to the conclusion a long time ago that with the gifts I was blessed with I could be either a super bad world-renowned pimp or steadfast hardnosed preacher. At my age it seems like I've been here before because I've been through it and seen a whole lot. My thoughts drift frequently, and some people might call me crazy if they knew all the things that swirled around in this crazy head of mine.

The scripture for the day was: *Jesus answered and said unto them, Ye do err, not knowing the scriptures, nor the power of God* (Matthew 22:29). As far as this applying to me, I know I have many errors in my ways. Anytime that a man knows God's word and disobeys or chooses to ignore it, he will fail. Knowing this, it's ludicrous for me not to follow Him. My problem is that although I have seen and experienced His magnificent power in the past, I forget to remember (probably due to the weed) that He is not slack in His promises.

Throughout the years I have really had problems with lusting after women and material possessions. I always wanted to be "the man" coming up, although people have always naturally been drawn to me. For the most part the smoking causes me to withdraw from people and I become a very introverted person who doesn't seem to have a whole lot of personality. Those who know me know that I am full of life and personality, and that's probably why it saddens them that I smoke. I am on something new now though and that's why I invited you along cause I know it ain't gone be easy. It should really be a trip because I know Satan wants me just as bad as God, because I am a very influential worker and natural born leader. I know Satan ain't gone wanna give one of his best workers up that easy. I have turned so many young ladies out and made so many guys wanna be like me that it makes no sense. I will have to pay for my actions one day. I just hope God has mercy on me.

Oh yeah this is day one and it has begun quite smooth obviously because I have time to type and the fire is still lit in me from last night. This morning I smoked the short of the Black and Mild I had from last night while on the toilet and decided that it's do or die with this situation cause I may not have much time. I took the weed that I had leftover in my pipe from last night, dumped it in the toilet and flushed it, so when I get off work I won't fall into my pattern of getting off and smoking my free time away. So I am feeling good about that because I made the right choice.

1:11 p.m. 7/26/04 Front Desk
Since I last left, I've been having an IM conversation with an ex-coworker named Nia. She is a preacher's kid and loves the church but doesn't have all the knowledge she needs to have. When I challenge her thinking, she refers to her friends and family to reaffirm what she believes and to help her find and define what she believes. Anyway we have been talking about female preachers

and I've showed her the scriptures that say that they shouldn't do it, but she is too stuck on what she's been told all of her life to take a step back and really look at it, I believe. I wasn't pressuring her or trying to prove I was right. I was just allowing her to find what she thought would prove me wrong. Needless to say, I am still waiting. She enlisted her friend, her brother, and I don't know who else. It's hard trying to fight the Bible or even argue with it. That is what I think is making it difficult for them because they aren't arguing with me. They are arguing with the Bible because it clearly states in 1 Timothy 2:10-12, *Let the woman learn in silence with all subjection. But I suffer not a woman to teach, nor to usurp authority over the man, but to be in silence. For Adam was first formed, then Eve.* It's hard to interpret that any other way with the other scriptures that I gave her. I feel good because I seized an opportunity and redeemed my time today. I'm still not finished, but I just thought I would fill you in on that little tidbit. Life is starting ...

10:50 p.m. 7/26/04 Violet's Room

So far so good. Day one was successful. I haven't smoked anything since that short of a Black and Mild I had before I went to work. Already God is showing me the opportunities available to me. I am so blessed, and today I was able to see a few quite clearly. I am pretty sure it doesn't get easier, but I am glad that I made it.

I also spoke with Nia and she said she enjoyed the conversation today about women preaching in the church. When I asked her if she found the verses she was looking for she admitted they weren't in there, basically telling me that she had no biblical evidence to back up why she thinks it isn't against God's will. I overstood earlier. Like I stated, people don't wanna hear the truth. I am wondering if she's going to be motivated to seek out the truth and find out for herself once and for all about what she believes or if she is just going to believe the things she's told without checking the info for herself. I know had it been me and someone challenged my beliefs with a ton of scriptures, I would really be inquiring about my beliefs and why I believe what I believe.

2

THE FIRST TEST

8:52 a.m. 7/27/04
I woke up feeling good although it was raining. I put on some rain clothes but inside I feel joy because I am ready to take on the world as I continue upon my journey. It's crazy, but on a side note . . . as I was walking to work when I got on campus there was no one even close to me or my path to work, but all of a sudden the smell of chronic jumped into my nostrils. It wasn't just the smell of huff. It smelled like that ooohhhwee. Anyway, I thought that was funny cause when I looked around there was NO POSSIBLE WAY that it could have happened. Anyway, sometimes your mind plays tricks on you.

I think I am going to stay busy today because I have filing to do. I am going to try to pay my bills while at work and hold a convo when I can with Mrs. Nia. Talk about multitasking. Now that I have my family van fixed (Thank God!) I can finally start going back to church on the regular. I also am going to try to find the time to stop somewhere and grab a couple composition notebooks so that I can write too. Although I prefer to type, who knows when I may feel like writing. Niggaz have tore up the majority of the computers in the computer lab where I stay. They stole mouses, jammed disk drives, downloaded viruses ... Niggaz. That would leave me with either writing by hand or typing on Violet's laptop. God bless the child that got his own. I think if I had my own laptop, I could easily write a book about my life or probably would have done it by now if it wasn't for that darn smoking.

Violet is real ... what's the word I'm looking for ... hmmm ... I'm not sure, but she has a lot of rules and boundaries that a lot of times clashes with my personality because I'm a free spirit and she is like this rule freak. Anyway, I don't think that is going to work out too much longer, so that's why I need the books.

I was reading the book that I used to read in the morning just to keep my mind right before I started the day called *Reclaim Your Power* by a black man named Terrance Dean. He went through some crap in his lifetime! It's like inspirational messages for the day so I decided I would read it again only this time actually doing the little exercises in my journal. It is supposed to be a 30-day guide to hope, healing and inspiration for men of color. Day 1's topic was to listen and I think I did that pretty good in the convo with Nia. The exercise ironically was to make a list of the times when the Spirit was guiding you and you ignored it. Evidently, I've been doing that for a while too, but I spoke on that yesterday.

Day 2: Be still. That was the message for today, be still and let the Spirit dwell in you. That's funny considering the plans for all that *I* thought I had to do today and tonight. Maybe this is the Spirit trying to tell me something today, right now. We will see how it pans out. I will try my best to be still today and we will see what happens. Only thing is, I don't want to be idle and I am working on redeeming the time. That's why I was trying to get those things done today because I have been procrastinating, being still, doing nothing as of late. I think it's funny how that's the message and how it conflicts with what I had planned.

This is getting interesting. Can I drop what I think I should do and let the Spirit guide me? We will see. The exercise for today is to list the things that prevent me from being still and how can I start being still today. Hmm. Things that prevent me from being still: my cell phone, having to go smoke, my stereo, the company I keep, and being so hungry that my stomach is touching. When I'm high I am very still. How big of a contradiction is that? That's usually when I'm listening and open and more inclined to pay attention to myself and the things going on in my head. I know that's crazy but as of late I was being real still. I would call it lazy, getting high smoking and just chilling not doing much maybe watching a DVD and just relaxing . . . eventually going to sleep or taking long naps. How still can you get? Lol! Anyway I just thought that was real funny, but I do know that it is hard for God to communicate with you even if you are being still when your mind is cluttered.

Half the time when I was high I couldn't tell if some of my thoughts were from God and the Holy Spirit or from Satan himself. One minute I would be thinking something positive and the next I would be planning what I would say and how I was going to evade somebody's daughter's most sacred and private space. Anyway, the other part asks how can I start being still today? Good question! You tell me, naw but for real let's see . . . I think by eliminating the music I listen to and just having a quiet day, that may help my mind be more at ease and help my spirit be still. Other than that I don't know cause I gots to keep it moving. Now am I disobeying the Spirit? I don't think so, but thanks for accompanying me on this journey. We will see . . .

11:21 a.m. 7/27/04
I am currently talking to Charlene on Yahoo Instant Messenger. She's at work like me and I think God is presenting me with another opportunity. She's telling me some things that Missy has told her about her family and her illness and it is kind of scary because I know Missy loves me and would jump at the opportunity to marry me. She brings it up all the time, but I brush it off like I do with other girls who may come to love me. Anyway, I am finding out that her family is not real supportive although they seemed like they were there for her when she flew me into Nebraska. Now that I understand the seriousness of her illness, it helps me to *overstand* her sense of urgency in moving this relationship along.

She flew to Chi-town for my family reunion about two weeks ago and she already talking bout coming to see me again on her B-Day and on graduation in May. I think she is afraid of the future and whether she is going to die or not. Earlier I was thinking I really don't wanna be slowed down again, but I feel like I have an obligation as a Christian to be there for this young lady in her time of need. This is where God comes in, because I know some of her beliefs are unchallenged and based on falsehoods, but I never really felt compelled to rock the boat. Why? I'm not sure maybe because I can't really see myself married to her because she's not all that spiritual as a person and I need a spiritual goddess to ride with me, with all the thoughts that go through my head. Anyway, I believe it is time to tell her the truth and introduce her to my heavenly father. I am going to start teaching her so she has some real deal insurance and not the man made insurance, and of course with the real deal insurance comes assurance.

Today's scripture of the day on Bible.com: *There is a way that seemeth right unto a man, but the end thereof are the ways of death* (Proverbs 16:25). I had to think about this one awhile, not because I don't know what it means, but because I am trying to apply these scriptures to my life. Rather than being a reader and hearer of the word, I wanna be a doer and apply it to my life right now. Before I can give an analysis though, I got to be still and let something come to me, cause right now my thoughts are scattered. Like trying to pimp Missy would lead to destruction. That's what my mom was preaching to me earlier this week. It also could be applying as far as I see it in my life to some of the ladies I am pursuing. So I guess I am going to chill, but just in case I didn't tell you, let me fill you in: That is a major task for me because I could have sex all day long if time permitted me. I have been told, and I guess you can say (even though it is cocky), that I am good at it.

This is a major part of the struggle that I am embarking upon because I know you can't serve or love two masters, and my love for women is strictly of Satan. It's me giving into temptation, simple as that, because of course if you pimpish you can't love 'em and I can't remember the names of most of the girls I have had sex with. That's why I keep a picture album, old letters and cards so I can remember. Oh yeah, marijuana affects the brain . . . Message! Anyway I know I am going to have to work on this because you can't love anything more than God if you wanna please Him, so I pray that He continues to be merciful and guide my steps and my thoughts because it is all conceived in the mind with one lustful thought. Anyway, I think I've given enough meat for one entry so I'm going to get back to work.

For lunch I went back to the crib and caught a nap cause I was feeling fatigued from being up with my neighbor last night. I think that is a waste of time, but she did take me to church and the art museum so I'll hang around cause it keeps me from doing some of the things I used to do. Just as I figured, there hasn't been any conversation between me and my ex-coworker and eventually I'll have to face the music and realize that she got some growing to do to catch my mental capacity. Some things she just can't handle, almost as if she's been brainwashed and can't accept anything out of the regularly scheduled program that she was given. She doesn't even have the desire to know the truth and it saddens me sometimes that people can be like that. Hopefully, God will use me to bring some of these people to see the light when I get my mind right.

I'm not sure if I have a whole lot to talk about because I am just trying to be still and feel whatever it is I am supposed to feel. I can say I am sleepy, and that is without smoking my traditional Black, but I got to keep it moving too. Big contradiction, huh? I told you I can be complex. How am I trying to be still and keep it moving at the same time? Don't ask me, but I need to pay my rent and these bills and now that I have the money, thanks to the almighty, I want to pay them and get them out of the way. If I sit too still I might fall asleep cause I have been yawning all morning, but I ain't down like I used to be had it been fatigue from smoking. I don't want to go to sleep cause I want to go to men's class tonight at church at 7:30 so that don't leave me too much time to sleep in between getting off work at 5, paying bills and napping til about 6:45. I miss the joy I get when in His sanctuary, almost as if that is my real home.

3

BRO. DASHINGS AND THE CHURCH

9:03 a.m. 7/28/04
Boy, I got plenty to talk about now. First off, I went to men's study last night and it felt great to be in the fellowship of the brotherhood. Last night we talked about living in the world but not being like the world. It was a very interesting study because there was a new teacher who challenged those in the class to back up their responses with biblical answers. I was extremely happy that I was there because like I said yesterday, I was tired and I was scared I was going to nap and miss getting up. Well the Lord blessed me with the strength to keep going and I paid my bills and rent, so I knew I had to go give Him the glory. When I walked outside to go to the van, it started pouring all of a sudden with the sun shining bright! How 'bout that as encouragement to keep going? Plus, I had my new Adidas on. It rained harder as I decided that the rain wasn't going to stop me. It was almost as if Satan was telling me "Man, it ain't worth it right now. You can go tomorrow when it ain't raining." Well I made the right choice and persevered on, so

I was happy that I won that battle. Sitting in class, I was filled with joy and couldn't contain it, so I had to speak up and participate in the discussion. It felt good because a lot of the brothers knew who I was and embraced me as such.

When leaving men's class it was still pouring and the roads were super bad. I can say last night was one time that I was glad I had the family van because there was a flood warning for the city and it was hell on those stuck out in the rain trying to get home. The streets were flooded bad and a lot of times because it was so dark, you couldn't see it until you got in the middle of a huge puddle and splashed through the water. There were so many cars creeping through the puddles and others sitting on the side of the road with their hazards on. It was a wonderful experience for me because I knew I was going to make it home safely because I was out doing God's will, so He was going to see me through it. With that said I was getting it on that highway! While people were creeping, I was seeking! Seeking room to squeeze by them and continue on my journey, usually splashing huge waves of water on those cars which blocked my way for too long. The minivan was brilliant, trailblazing through the streets and because it is so heavy I felt like I was driving a tank through those little puddles.

Bro. Dashings was one of the first truly genuine people that I met at this church. He's introduced me to his family, showed me where he lives, invited me over to hang out and run with him, given me all his numbers, and I still haven't taken advantage of his Christian fellowship. Well things are about to change because tonight I am going to call him and I am going to start checking up on him.

With all of that said Day 2 was a complete success! No smoking, none whatsoever! Last night I missed the journal entry because I started listening to Bro. Crunk's tape and playing Cleveland versus Denver on NBA LIVE. Bro. Crunk is the preacher who was preaching at a gospel meeting that my mom went to and she has been telling me I need to listen to the tapes, so to keep other thoughts out like thoughts of boredom, I popped it in and listened as I played the game. It actually wasn't a bad combination. After that game and another one, I got a surprise visit from one of my female associates who I haven't seen in a long time. She has been on a "sexual hiatus" or at least that's what she told me. I don't know though because she seemed pretty lonely last night. We ended up watching *Dodgeball* until about 1:30 a.m.

I learned something from her last night—which is rare for me to learn anything worth knowing from the company I keep, because on the low they all aren't the brightest crayons in the box. Anyway, she revealed to me that Sen. Kerry's wife used to be married to a Republican senator before her ex-husband died, most likely killed, in a plane crash. Now she is married to a Democrat, but most of her money is tied in with the Republicans and I'm sure she has Republican values. My feelings on this is the New World Order and the Illuminati folks have put us in a bad situation. Either way they win, and their agenda is moved forward with Bush or Kerry. We as the American People have no choice. They have already begun to take over. First, they stole an election then they bamboozled people into voting for the same agenda just under different parties. Anyway, that sucks. That's why I might just vote for Ralph Nader, although I'm scared to do that because Bush may win again, and Bush is already cocky he doesn't need or deserve another go at it.

Anyway, Day 3 has started and once again I am prepared to face the challenges that may lie ahead. The message for Day 3 in *Reclaim Your Power* is to show kindness. This is something I think I do on a regular basis so that should be no problem. The exercise calls to make a list of people who can benefit from your kindness. Well before I started this morning's entry, I walked downstairs to help my supervisor Mrs. Michael bring up bags of food for Dr. Gulley's luncheon today. Dr. Gulley is the token white woman who works here. She's already got a PhD, but for some reason she's been here dealing with the dysfunction for the past two years. She is transferring to Virginia Tech and today is her last day, so we are having a luncheon for her. Anyway, I always show kindness, but the one person who some kindness could benefit and to whom it would actually be a task to show kindness is Mrs. Chanel, and she ain't here today. She called in sick, but I know the truth.

11:11 p.m. 7/28/04 Violet's Room

Tonight, I went to church and I feel great! Brother Dashings came and got me and we had a wonderful talk. I think that he is just the brother who I need to work with in terms of fellowshipping and pulling myself away from some of the people who I don't need to be around. The lesson in class tonight came from James 1:14-19. It was dealing with how men are not tempted by God but are drawn away by their own lusts. We basically discussed how when we sin we make the choice to turn our back on God, therefore separating ourselves from Him. It was very relevant to me and my situation.

When I started this journal, I thought it was going to be about smoking, but ever since I made up my mind that I was going to stop and I documented it in my journal I haven't had the urge. I haven't smoked at all today, but I am fatigued again because I didn't get to sleep last night until late. I spoke with Missy and she is doing all right but her phone got turned off so she shouldn't be calling me as often now.

Oh, good news! More blessings have come my way. ESPN called me while I was trying to sneak in a nap before I called Brother Dashings for church. I was kind of caught off guard, but I'm sure that the guy I spoke with concerning the job sensed the excitement in my voice. He explained that they were impressed by my resume and possibly had a position for me. I was caught off guard, but I still was able to explain that I was in school and would be done in May. We exchanged contact information and agreed to stay in contact, because it has always been a dream of mine to work for ESPN. Even though I was still sleepy, I did convey that message to him quite clearly. He agreed to email me info and keep me posted when positions opened up.

I may have some struggles to document coming soon because I found out today that I have negative two hundred something dollars in the bank. I will be budgeting something seriously the rest of this week. I left work early today just because. Oh, and Mrs. Michael know not to mess with me because I fixed the printer and I did it my way. Now the new printer is setup to print labels just like I said and it didn't even take me that long. I was still kind by the way. Instead of throwing the fact that I had fixed it in her face, I helped her clean up after the luncheon before I left work. She was trying to offer me all kinds of food. Whoever said you kill evil with love was right.

Quin called but I didn't answer. Why, I don't know, but I figure she is trying to invite me to her graduation and I would love to attend, I just hope that circumstances permit me to go. It would be wonderful to see Quin again. She's one of my friends from undergrad at Jackson State. She's the definition of a Chi-town chick—slick talking, dress to the nines, freaky and a "bout it bout it" female. She is so down to earth and real it makes no sense. She used to open up the door for a nigga late at night or early in the morning after I had got high and went to the club or had been out with some chick.

4

NIA'S LATE AND HATERS GONE HATE

8:28 a.m. 7/30/04 School of Graduate Studies
The song that I chose to listen to as I type this morning is "Footprints" by Young Buck of G-Unit. The hook goes "Walk with me, Lord. First there was two sets of footprints in the sand and then there was one set of footprints in the sand. When times get hard and things hit the fan, God don't walk with me – He carry me, man." I'm feeling some kind of way . . . First off, I'm at work early because of Mrs. Chanel and her evil spirit, or at least that's the way I see it. I must say though God is good because He allowed me to wake up this morning and make it here on time. I also actually got a chance to eat breakfast so the day started cool. Nia called me early, like 7 a.m., talking about she's late. I knew what she was talking about from the jump, but I just laid there and listened to see what she had to say. Thing is, I never came in her so that should be a miracle baby! I've been sensing something with her ever since I got back from Milwaukee. She says she's going to call me later and let me know what's up, so you know I look forward

to that. I don't know what to think about her, but I know my heart has been talking to me about her for a while. For some reason I was getting the feeling that she was cheating or had forgot about me even while I was in Milwaukee. That's why I called her while I was there. Yesterday I called her and told her about ESPN wanting to fly me in because she had encouraged me to go ahead and apply anyway when I was thinking about not applying. So I felt it only right to tell her since she's asked me on several occasions had I heard anything. Funny thing is when I told her about it, she said I knew you were special (sort of like *yeah, I got a good one*). I don't think she meant it that way, but that was the way I saw it, almost like a warning that from here on out I gotta be careful because when a chick knows you going places, they tend to want to hold on anyway they can. That's why this morning's call didn't surprise me really, because I knew. I had been feeling something, I just couldn't explain it. I still am not worried. I am so glad I was smart and wasn't completely caught up where I would lose my senses.

Moving on, last night was my first test and I passed! I was really set to spend my time updating my NBA live rosters, but P called early talking bout he got five days off. He asked me what was going on my way and I told that fool nothing, and he still decided that he was going to come over. I went to the liquor store with him because I knew I wasn't getting anything and I wanted to kick his tail in the game, but when we got there we seen a mutual acquaintance, Herb. We ended up going over to his house where everyone was drinking and smoking except for me. I felt so good! I ended up leaving to walk home so I could get my hair braided. As I figured, that nigga P is selfish and didn't bother to remove me from the situation even though I mentioned to him before we even left that I wasn't trying to do the things I used to do. Instead of him taking me home when I asked, he sat and procrastinated so I got up and decided I would walk.

Loban wondered why I was walking and I explained there was nothing there for me since I was trying not to smoke, and this nigga all of a sudden just let some hate out that I would never have expected. When he tried to stop, I never mocked him or tried to discourage him, but he felt the need to put me on the spot, so I just let it go in one ear and out the other and continued on my journey home. He probably hating because it didn't work out for him. It's really no big deal for him though cause his parents are paying for his rent, so I don't think he really tripping. That was the Spirit leading me to the truth about the two characters who I hang out with probably the most. Neither wants to see me shine, so you know what that means: time to distance myself from the lames.

11:29 a.m. 7/30/04
I feel so much better. I have calmed down in my spirit and I am not angry now. I did research on the ESPN job and printed out plenty of tips to help me with the interview, which means I won't be bored tonight if I redeem my time and read up and prepare. I still haven't spoken with Charlene yet, but I am after this entry. I tried to get a good portion of my work out the way just in case Hen come in being nosey I will have plenty to show her. I also did my inspirational reading and read some scriptures. That reminds me . . . tonight I'm determined to clean up my crib and listen to one of the gospel tapes with Brother Crunk preaching.

The scripture for the day is: *If any of you lack wisdom, let him ask of God, that giveth to all men liberally, and upbraideth not; and it shall be given him* (James 1:5). That is a good scripture and I believed that when I was a lil shorty, so I used to pray for wisdom. God does answer prayers because He allowed me to be challenged and questioned to the point where I wanted to find out the truth for myself. Anyway, I will apply that by going to God and asking Him to be with me during this whole interviewing process. I pray He will give me the wisdom to know when to speak and when to be silent and listen. Speaking of wisdom, I miss Grandad because he always tried to instill wisdom and the truth about God's word in me whenever I came around. If you are listening, Dad Hill, I love you.

I spoke with Granny the other night and it just so happened that she was crying when I called and I could hear it in her voice. She had been left all alone and she was lonely. I spoke with her for a while on my way back to church, but I know I gotta call her more often because she really don't have nobody. I am getting sleepier as the time passes, even though Nia brought me a Mountain Dew.

The message for Day 5 from *Reclaim Your Power* is trust yourself. I think I have to trust myself on this interview. No matter how many people say this is the opportunity of a lifetime that only comes around once in a person's life, I have to trust myself and my own instincts and decide whether or not I want this job. That's like the Spirit sending me a message because I knew my family was going to say take it, but I want my degree. I worked hard and suffered for it and I want my lil piece of paper. Well for now I am fighting to stay awake, so I am going to get on IM to generate some conversation.

4:41 p.m. 7/30/04 School of Graduate Studies

Today was a pretty good day. I resisted Satan as far as the internet is concerned, no porn and not too much BlackPlanet.[3] No one really came back and bothered me today, so it was a good day. I got my work done and I even finished some work for Dr. Tailor. I also spoke with Nia and dig this: She said she knows that she is pregnant because she went and took a test. We spoke during my lunch break, and she, of all people, told me she was going to have an abortion—the black Republican who told me she was voting for Bush because he was man or "Christian enough to stand against abortion and gay marriages." I thought that was very ironic and couldn't help but to mention it to her. She remembered that she said it and agreed with me that you never know about certain situations and issues until things happen to you. I am kind of skeptical of the whole situation although I told her I support her in whatever she decides to do because it takes two. I am skeptical because the Spirit was trying to tell me something was wrong

---

3 BlackPlanet is an African-American social networking service.

a couple weeks back when I was at home in the Mill and I hadn't heard from her in a while.

I got mad love for her and I would hate to lose her as a friend. I think I could teach her a couple things about the gospel, but, like I said earlier, my intuition is rarely wrong and I have learned to pay attention to it when it calls me for my attention. The weekend is coming up and I'm sure the real trials and tribulations are about to start. Pray for me.

5

NIA'S ULTIMATUM AND HERB'S HOUSE

8:41 a.m. 8/2/04 School of Graduate Studies
This morning started off good, because I actually got up when my alarm went off even though I didn't get much sleep. Funny thing happened to me last night. I dreamed somehow, someway that I was riding with Kanye West talking about life. I mentioned to him that I admired him for having the courage to rap about some of the things he rapped about. How I got there I don't remember, but from that point on I was conscious and wasn't in R.E.M. sleep anymore. It felt as if I was controlling the dream. I let him know that I used to rap but had put it on the backburner because I was waiting on my calling from God. He asked to hear something of mine, and I told him I didn't memorize any of my raps cause I used to smoke so much weed but that my freestyles were spectacular or real, depending on what was on my heart. Kanye proceeded to tell me that he wanted to hear me freestyle cause he wanted to know why I gave it up and that he had just finished two beats that he wanted me to hear. So he played the beats and

I begin to freestyle, but what was so surreal was that my mind was actually working and I was actually freestyling in my mind like I was doing it for him. It was tight if I must say so myself. It was also very relevant, although I don't remember any lines. I talked about how life was, how brave Kanye was for changing the game, how other rappers were selling their soul and selling their people out for the almighty buck.

Without missing a beat, at about 5 in the morning, my mind was freestyling and I was going to stop in the dream after the first beat went off, but Kanye had pulled a tape recorder out and was geeking and said keep it going. I ended up flowing all the way through his second beat too cause I was feeling it. After I finished freestyling for about two minutes without stumbling, Kanye was like, "Yo man, you the truth." I rapped about putting rap on the backburner because I wasn't sure if that was what God wanted me to do and I didn't see a way to awake people to the issues and situations that they faced through rap. I was basically dropping knowledge about what I had learned through my experiences in life and where I saw the industry, other rappers and the world headed.

We were riding in Kanye's Range and he got on the phone and was like, "Yo, I got the real Hov. I'm coming through." After he got off, he told me we were going to see Hov and Dame. So we went to a studio and they met us outside in the parking lot and Kanye played his beats and was like spit the truth. With totally different things on my heart, it was like God took over my mind and I begin to spit about how I liked Hov but didn't consider him to be all the way real cause he had all this influence and knew niggaz in the industry was trying to be like him and instead of using this power for good he was leading niggaz to sell their soul for the almighty dollar and how the white man was going to look out for him for that. Instead of stopping me, they let me continue rhyming and then somewhere in the freestyle I jumped to Dame and talked about how he was on the David Chappelle show and how I respected him more after that cause he wasn't too high to act a clown and make fun of himself, but I rhymed the scheme with clown and how at that moment his true inner self he found or something like that. Dame just looked at me like *this kid is the truth*, while Hov kept the same game face on.

After I finished, Hov hugged me and said, "I respect your gangster to the fullest cause you the first nigga who auditioned for me and had the nuts to talk about me in the rap, and it was all real and true. I don't know how you know, but I've been dealing with that issue for a while and that's part of the reason I retired." Dame was like, "Word, son. You are the truth! We signing you. Word is bond." I then explained to them that I really wasn't a rapper who could sit down and pen some classic ish. It was just whatever God had on my heart at the time that I could spit. I told them I could do cameos on conscious songs and interlude spits, but I talked about how it was God who put the words on my heart and they were just in awe. Dame talked about how they would market me and my contract and the business side while Hov was silent. He wanted to sign me to his label cause that was the way he was trying to go in music, to a more conscious and grown up audience. He wanted to start a new hip-hop movement similar to the civil rights where people had to respect artists as more than just rappers but great leaders, and he'd brought Kanye in the game to help start that movement.

I was conscious through all of this and it seemed funny, but eventually I drifted back to sleep after Hov told me that cause I don't remember much after that. I just remember that I dropped two dope long freestyles in my sleep and it really felt like God had put the words in my heart cause I really was flowing that early in the morning flawlessly with only an imaginary beat in my head! How bout that?

Anyway, since I put on yesterday's clothes, I had extra time in the shower to talk with God, read my Bible and listen to one of the sermons on tape that I got. I am going to check some emails and read my inspirational message and scripture of the day.

10:03 a.m. 8/2/04 School of Graduate Studies

I just got finished checking my emails and reading my inspirational thoughts. This is Day 6 in *Reclaim your Power* and the message of the day is to be unpredictable and spontaneous. I think for the most part I am, but I am trying to think of a way that I could do this or apply this to my life today specifically. The book gave some examples, but I really don't see them applying to me right now because of various reasons. The main one might be because I'm feeling lazy today and I plan on sleeping good. The exercise is to list all the things that I have always thought of doing and to write the ways I can be unpredictable and spontaneous in my life. One way I could do this is by sparking up a godly conversation in some of the ungodly places I have been as of late to see where people heads are at. I also did something spontaneous by writing Lala an email and telling her basically that I hope things are going well with her, she was in my spirit and that I wasn't trying to be enemies. She really was in my spirit and usually I suppress it, but I thought what the heck. I'll let her know that I still got love for her although I am not in love with her. I think that's being spontaneous enough for the day.

The scripture for the day is *The fear of the LORD is the beginning of knowledge: but fools despise wisdom and instruction* (Proverbs 1:7). This is a good scripture because it is one of them that I have come across in my life many a time. As a child because my pops really wasn't trying to teach me much, I used to read proverbs because Mom and Dad Hill and all the rest of my spiritual mentors used to tell me that Proverbs teaches you how to be a man, so I listened and made sure to try to know the principles in Proverbs. I tried to engrave them in my heart and I believe that it worked cause when I'm around foolishness I just can't stand it unless I'm high. That was probably the reason I smoked so much, because the people I find myself associating with are rarely on my level. We might see eye to eye on a couple of issues but never on the same level. Anyway, that is a good scripture. My mind is really fatigued right now and I am fighting sleep so I am going to end this journal entry and do some work and hopefully that will help to reenergize my mind.

5:03 p.m. 8/2/04 School of Graduate Studies

I am sooo tired it makes no sense. I've been holed up here in the back just trying to make it through the day. At lunch I went to the Morgan View office and found out that my package from Sheila had arrived last week. When I first had got back from lunch I glanced at the books and they look real helpful. Boy, I tell you . . . niggaz need help these days. ESPN's HR department didn't call today; that was a disappointment. I hope I haven't stuck my foot in my mouth by telling everybody too early. That has happened to me many times in life and you'd think I'd learn my lesson. I've been dealing with disappointment all my life so it comes as nothing new when it does happen. God is good though. Hopefully tonight I will better be able to recall the events and happenings of the day cause as of right now I am out of it. Guess I gotta work on getting in the bed at a decent time cause this is ridiculous. I just thank God for allowing me to make it through the day.

6
LALA'S EMAIL

9:51 a.m. 8/3/04 School of Graduate Studies
Here's Lala's response to the email I sent her the other day:

Charlie~

It's funny that you wrote . . . You have been on my mind also it's crazy cause I had a dream (or nightmare depending upon what perspective you take) about you the other night. But anyhow I'm doing good preparing for my last year trying to get things in order spiritually, mentally and physically so I've been extremely busy. I still haven't completely unpacked from Europe. Well anyhow I hope you are doing well also and best wishes to you as you finish up school and in other aspects of your life. As far as being enemies . . . I'm past that. I'm too old to have some juvenile grudge and walk around hating people. What's done is done . . . stuff happens so deal with it and let it go.

Ms. Jones

From: Me
To: Her

> *What's up Buddy? Long time no chat, I hope things are going well with U. U were on my heart last night and I wanted to call U but then again I didn't cause I didn't want to "rock the boat." I hope things are going well with U, and I wish U the best. Just know that your boy still thinks about U and I still got luv for U. I might have strange ways of showing it, but I still do care about U and even though we may not be the best of friends, lovers or whatever I still desire to have some type of relationship and communication with U as long as U can handle it. All I know is I don't want to be enemies and I don't want it to be where if I bump into U anywhere that it is awkward or uncomfortable. Anyway I hope this doesn't cause a major riff or whatever in your life or day. I just had this in my spirit and had to release it.*

So that went well and believe you me, I am glad about that cause I put that girl through hell even though I loved her. What made me write her was I was going through some emails yesterday and I stumbled upon this:

I wasn't going to bring it up . . . I was trying to push it out of my mind but I can't. When u told me the other day that you were still doubting the whole situation it hurt and then bringing it up again in the email hurt again. I tried to tell myself that it didn't matter what you or anyone else thought (and it doesn't) because I know the truth about the baby and you know because you saw the test, but most importantly God knows. But for you not to believe me is like a slap in the face. It still hurts my heart to know that I didn't have your trust or that you would think of me in that way (a liar). Then I tried to tell myself that was just your way of dealing with the situation because you never believed me when I told you I was pregnant before until you saw it in writing or saw the ultrasound. I just don't understand it. Why you think I would lie? I wasn't trying to keep you around. I told you I didn't need your help and I never asked you to give me help financially so I'm not understanding what u thought my basis for lying would be. We weren't getting along and a baby would have made it worse. That's why I didn't want you around if I would have kept the baby. ANYWAY I know I'm rambling in parts but I think you can get the gist. When you brought that up again it made me feel like it was happening all over again. I was dealing with the pain of you not being there cause you don't trust me and the pain of losing not one of our kids but losing four.

Needless to say that really hit my heart, and yes I am airing out some dirty laundry, but it is good because once I tell you, then it's like releasing a deep dark secret and a huge weight is lifted from my conscience and my shoulders. Anyway, enough about Lala for now. That was why I started this entry so late cause I was off on some other stuff. Last night I actually was good and made it to bed before 1:30, but for some strange reason I still feel kind of drowsy. I also am semi-stopped up as if I had been smoking, but of course I wasn't.

I went by Camel and Co. house after my journal entry and clowned with them for a while. They wasn't really doing nothing but sitting around on the phone and doing what girls with no life do. Afterwards I went to Sherman Merman's and beat down the door but she didn't answer, so I am figuring that she is back taking sleeping pills to fall asleep. I am going to have to talk to her about that. From there I proceeded back to Violet's room to get the new *VIBE* so I could read it on the toilet cause by that time the spaghetti was talking to me. From the toilet I took Violet her book back and went and got in the bed.

No smoking in any part of that day or night. Which brings us to today. Day 7 in *Reclaim Your Power* is Be Responsible. The exercise asks in what ways have you not been responsible for your life? That is an easy one for me. I haven't been responsible by smoking my life away. Because of smoking I have missed valuable opportunities to learn things, go places and meet people. I have hid my light by smoking, therefore not having to own up to the responsibility of being blessed with sooo much. What can I do to take responsibility for my life? Set goals, keep my eyes open and my spirit in tune to the opportunities that God blesses me with so I can advance and be successful. Oh, and keep it real with myself and God. If I don't keep it real with nobody else, I gotta remember who I am and whose I am.

The scripture for the day from Bible.com is: *But ye shall receive power, after that the Holy Ghost is come upon you: and ye shall be witnesses unto me both in Jerusalem, and in all Judaea, and in Samaria, and unto the uttermost part of the earth* (Acts 1:8). I believe I can apply this to my life by telling people how good God is when they ask me how I'm doing. I have to show through my actions and deeds that no matter what, I can rejoice because I know He is good and will bring me out of whatever storm or fog I may be in. This is easier said than done, but if I continue to work on it (and live it eventually), I will learn to be content in whatever state I am like Paul.

I really can't wait to go to church tonight and fellowship because I feel I need it. My morning started off great, because while eating breakfast I popped in the tape from Sheila, and Bro. Gains made me smile as soon as I heard his voice. Before his sermon he had the church join him in singing "By and By When the Morning Comes." It felt good to hear the congregation singing again.

Anyway, I am doing fine, no smoking and I am redeeming the time. Sometime today I am going to finish studying for the LSAT. Later.

3:34 p.m. 8/3/04 Front Desk

Today has been slow motion too. I must say I have been good today though, so I'm proud of myself. I think I may be going through withdrawal because I haven't been feeling high like I do when I get off work. I think work is stealing my joy because I am shut off from the world in a backroom. I have to find some way to appreciate this job. Speaking of jobs, Loban was coming in from an interview and said he finally found a job. I'm happy for that nigga cause he been looking awhile and an idle mind is the devil's playground. I thank God for this job cause it has provided me with a way to pay my rent. I did get my work done today though and I should be finished with a major task which I know no one expected me to finish before the deadline I set for myself.

I'll be leaving early today, thank God! That gives me time to take a nap before men's class. I hope Bro. Dashings is going cause I really don't have any gas. I look forward to getting my spirit fed and experiencing the fellowship of the brotherhood. I think I am feeling the effects of not being fed in church on Sunday morning. I just got off the phone with Charlene and her MSN account was just basically erased too. She reminded me about the Gmail account that she invited me to not too long ago.

While forwarding all my important emails to my new account I realized I got another response from my buddy Lala, and she sounds like she is in good spirits and has forgiven a nigga. She will be flying into Baltimore's airport sometime soon and wants to know if I can keep her company until her ride gets off work. Now how does that sound? She know better than that. I would be surprised if we can keep our hands off each other. Either way it would be good to see her cause I did love her, for real for real. I tried hard to just be with her. It was unfortunate what happened, but I grew and I believe she grew. Everything happens for a reason. I still haven't heard from the HR department at ESPN, so I am going to pray on that tonight.

10:51 p.m. 8/3/04 Morgan View Lab
God is Good! I made it to church and I even got my nap in. That makes it a good night fa sho! I also got a call from my nephews, Deuce Deuce and the Fatmack! That just made my day. Bro. Dashings came and got me for men's class, and we had a good class cause he taught it and everyone participated. It wasn't as many people in the class as it was last week, but I was just happy to see those there. We also got there early enough for the sweet hour of prayer, a 30-minute period where we all just thanked God for the blessings He bestowed upon us individually. It was only one person who thanked God for more than me. She went before me and was so happy and real with it that she started crying cause God has been so good to her. I went a few people after her and thanked God for her cause she basically gave me the green light to pour my heart out.

After church, while I was waiting on Bro. Dashings, I got on the phone and called Steve Mandy and ended up talking to Lil Lucky. He knew exactly who I was when he got on the phone and heard my voice. I talked with him for a while and he told me that he was doing good. He still in church and is going to be a freshman at Auburn in the fall. I knew he was going to make it out of Waynesboro, because it was too many before him who squandered the opportunity. Big Steve wasn't there, but I am sure I will get a chance to talk with him sooner or later. He helped me to stay sane while I was in Waynesboro and I will never forget him cause he was like a father to me. He taught me how to drive a stick in his brand new Eclipse and he used to let me floss. A young nigga really appreciated that, so when I make it and get some time, you know I gots to look him up. Lil Lucky said he got 15 Division 1 scholarship offers out of high school but chose Auburn because he could start playing his first year and have an immediate impact. So I'm going to have to keep track of him down there. I gave him my number and told him if he ever needed anything to let me know and I would see what I could do for him. He's probably going to be starting at safety so that gives me a reason to watch at least one team in college football this season. He actually sounded like he got his head on straight so I look for him to make it to the NFL. I knew he had it in him. The last time I cheered for him was at a pee wee football game that we all drove to. Anyway, it was good talking to him.

On the way back from church, Bro Dashings told me that one of the young ladies at church that night was his daughter and I didn't even know it, so I felt bad cause I kind of let the opportunity for a conversation go because I know me. She was thick and had I just started talking to her without knowing who she was, my mind may have started wandering and I may have flirted. Everything happens for a reason, so maybe next time . . .

Since I started the journal it really hasn't been a major issue, but this is another day in the book that I didn't smoke or even come close to smoking. God is good. I think my problem was trying to do it by myself and forgetting about from whence my help cometh. I'd really like to talk to Sheila, but she has no minutes and that sucks cause I know Sheila would set me straight about Lala and what I should and shouldn't do concerning her coming into town. Anyway, when I got something else to tell you, I will holla back. But until then . . .

*

At this point in my journey, I had already been reminded of or learned several lessons which now help me to walk in my purpose. I share and highlight these lessons hoping that they will help you in your walk.

First, I realized that God will often give way and allow you to live the way you want to live, even if that is separate and apart from Him, just so you can learn how much you need Him and how much He loves you. He will not force you to love Him, yet Romans 8:39 tells us nothing can separate us from His love. It is like the parable of the Prodigal Son. He was allowed by his loving father to go out and see what the world had to offer. Once the son learned some tough lessons or "came to his senses," he returned home where his father welcomed him with open arms despite his previous disrespect of his father. Similarly, once I returned to the church and started making a serious effort to do right, I came to my senses on a few things:

1. My worth wasn't in the things I possessed.
2. I had to distance myself from certain people, places and things that caused me to stumble and lose my balance.
3. I had to focus on trying to do good works instead of constantly pleasing my flesh.

4. Doing right requires some sacrifice.
5. The joy I was looking for could easily be found in simply resisting Satan and doing the right thing. God loved me so much that He answered my prayers and took the urge to smoke away from me so long as I was sober minded and focused on Him.
6. God will give you the strength that you need when you trust in Him and lean not on your own understanding. Proverbs 3 instructs us to trust in the Lord with all of our heart and acknowledge Him in all our ways and He will direct our path. I tried and failed several times in the past to get sober and do what I knew to be right. Each time I failed prior to this journey because I was depending on my own understanding and strength. James 1:5 instructs us to ask God for wisdom because He gives to all generously. Once I started seeking God's wisdom and guidance, He allowed me to see and finally recognize my frailty, my true character, the character of the people I hung around and why I found myself in certain situations. He also started to direct

my path to draw me closer to Him and a better life.

7. I learned that when you begin to walk in your purpose you should expect to be tested. Sometimes you don't know how strong or weak you are until you are tested. I learned that when you are trying to walk with God, you better understand that you will face many tests and you may even face some persecution. Furthermore, when you are trying to change, many people close to you may discourage you from changing for one reason or another. One of those reasons is because the old you benefits them in some way and they may not view the new you as being as beneficial. Oftentimes, persecution and some of your biggest tests will be by the hands of the ones closest to you.

Nia's pregnancy announcement was definitely a test. I didn't have the strength or wisdom to navigate that situation on my own and that could've caused me to seek comfort in smoking and familiar strongholds. While I didn't deal with that situation in the best manner, He still allowed me to navigate it without turning back to smoking.

Loban and P's failure to support me in my commitment not to smoke felt like persecution by those closest to me at the time. However, God comforted me during those times and the same God that comforted me will comfort you when your tests or persecutions arise if you trust Him, ask for wisdom and acknowledge Him in all your ways.

I will continue to be tested and face persecution throughout this book because I am still on my journey to walk in purpose. Just like my journey, your journey will be never-ending. God is not finished with us yet. I will always be a Christian warring against my flesh and the world until I hear "well done my good and faithful servant." During this time, I was depressed and beating myself up because of my poor decisions. Eventually, I began to realize God clearly doesn't call the qualified; He qualifies the called. God loves you and you are fearfully and wonderfully made. He can use you despite your flaws, just like He started to use me despite my many flaws (as you'll see in the coming entries).

For context going forward, I'd like to provide some insight on the women mentioned in the previous chapters that will feature prominently in what you are about to read. You already know about Nia, but please bear with me because it matters.

I met Violet while I was moving with my mom into my apartment at Morgan State and I relied on her for the duration of my matriculation. Violet was a faithful and reliable associate. I sometimes had a crush on her and then other times I couldn't stand her. We never were in a serious intimate relationship because she knew about the many girls I dealt with and she had too much self-respect to be one of many. Even though I was a chauvinistic jerk to her sometimes, she was typically there when I needed her.

I met Missy while I was a sophomore at Jackson State University. Missy and I immediately clicked back then because she was from Omaha, Nebraska, was a well-dressed thick girl who was built like a cheerleader, loved to wear Air Jordans and exclusive fitted baseball caps. To put it simply, Missy was fine with her own swag and had dudes chasing behind her all the time. She wasn't interested in corn balls as she would put it. She wanted a smart thug, so she stuck out from most of the girls who were chasing the corn balls who just happened to be frat dudes and athletes. Missy eventually was welcomed into my very small circle of friends while at Jackson State which is when we found out we had a lot in common.

Being from Omaha, Missy, like myself, always had to represent for her city because people who had never visited often joked about the percentage of black people living there. At a HBCU sometimes being from an unknown city comes with a lot of pressure to let folks know where you're from ain't sweet. I visited Missy in Omaha and I can tell you that like Milwaukee, ain't nothing sweet about the ghettos of Omaha. While Missy was at JSU, we often called her goofy because she was clumsy. I was the main one out of our crew that would tease her, but I only teased and joked about people that I liked. I later found out that Missy knew this. She had a crush on me, and I had a crush on her, but we never shared that with each other while we were at JSU. Perhaps it was because she was one of the few females that was considered part of the crew. However, our relationship grew deeper after Jackson State because she had to leave and didn't finish. She found out her clumsiness was a result of her having multiple sclerosis (MS). When she left JSU, Missy became lonely dealing with MS because she was confined to a wheelchair for the most part and didn't really have an active social life. We talked often and our friendship grew.

Sheila was a sweet Christian friend that I tried my best not to defile. She was a precious and rare jewel, a Chi-town virgin with a sweet soul and pretty brown eyes. I often shared with her my struggles in my relationship with my on and off again girlfriend at that time. We eventually developed a very strong relationship as I went on my journey to get sober.

Chanel was a very pretty young lady that I worked with at the Morgan State Graduate Student's Office. She had a rough upbringing in a different way. Although she was very pretty (which could've opened so many doors for her), she had a very ugly spirit and downright nasty attitude which turned people off. Looking back, I should thank God for her because her attitude was one of the key events that led to me applying for law school. An award that should've gone to Morgan was taken away because she had pissed some folks off. Eventually it was disclosed to me (because of the relationships I had formed) that Morgan didn't get a particular award because she had pissed the e-board off that was responsible for giving the award. Once that was disclosed, I let the e-board know that doing that was an injustice to the others who had worked hard. They eventually reversed their decision. The Dean of the Graduate School heard about what I did and suggested I go to law school, and the rest is history. She always acted like the world owed her because she had it rough coming up. She was a constant complainer and being around her would eventually drain you. I tried to counsel her and be a friend during my time at Morgan, but she was so toxic and off-putting that I eventually had to distance myself from her.

7

DEUCE MURDERED

8:59 a.m. 8/6/04 The School of Graduate Studies

I have mixed emotions and I can't say what type of day it is going to be, but so far it is a sad one. I am angry, pissed, curious, grateful, thankful and quiet in my spirit. This morning I had a rude awakening because Charlene called me and said someone had shot and killed Deuce. For some reason even though I knew she wouldn't joke about nothing like that, I told her to stop playing because I didn't wanna believe it. That hurt to hear her say that cause Deuce was my ace. Sad to say he has been more of a big brother and hood role model to me than my real brother Vick. I am going to miss him sorely.

Deuce was one of the only males beside my cousin Lil Landry who I made sure I looked up and went and saw every time I was home. Man, I'm going to miss Deuce. I was pissed this morning but for what I don't know. I wasn't pissed at God cause I know the good sometimes die young. I think I was pissed at whoever the hater was who took him out. It was a privilege to run with Deuce cause he was just real like that and people loved him all over the Mill. He also knew everybody cause he had been there all his life and had risen up to be a ghetto superstar, so I know it's gone be some drama. I just pray Cardi don't get involved.

I held him dear to my heart, but I couldn't even shed a tear for my man. I even tried, but all I could do was get angry at myself for not sharing the gospel with him. Deuce was a good dude. Although he sold dope for most of his life, he had turned that money into a legal car wash where he gave jobs to guys down and out, mainly hypes[4] but still. He raised my nephews when Vick wouldn't and not many men are going to raise someone else's kids. Poor Fat Mack. He called Deuce dad, so I know he is going to be devastated. All he got is me now cause he stopped looking to Vick after he lied to him so many times, talking bout he was gone come and get them to spend the night and they always ended up with their uncle. Man, I'm going to miss Deuce.

Day 10 in *Reclaim Your Power* and the theme is be a part of your community. At home, I tried to do this by befriending those in the hood who really didn't have friends and because I'm seen as being a super cool nigga. I like to think I actually

---

[4] A hype is essentially a narcotic addict. In Milwaukee we sometimes refer to them as dope fiends or crackheads.

made their life easier. Happy Man[5] is a great example cause niggaz don't really dog him out like they used to when I come home cause they know I mess with him and if they try to front on him or dog him out in front of me then I'm doggin them. And none of them niggaz in the hood gone dog me cause they know they can't. I'm well-traveled and smart, so these hating ass niggaz can only look at me with hatred in their eyes, but they gotta respect it cause they can't check it. I'm sorry, forgive me. That's that anger coming out and I don't need to revert back there.

Now for the scripture of the day: *But be ye doers of the word, and not hearers only, deceiving your own selves* (James 1:22). Now that is a good one. How ironic? Had I been a doer and not just a hearer, I might have somehow someway helped my man influence his ignorant brother to change his ways and slow down. And to think I smoked blunts with that dude . . . I'm soo hurt. I am trying to take my mind off all this negative ish, but it is sitting right there. Missy called me last night like a

---

5 Happy Man, as the hood affectionately called him, was a physically and mentally disabled person whose crack-addicted mother allowed him to roam the hood and stay out all day doing whatever. He always smelled like crap, his mouth was jacked up and his clothes were often soiled with a stench. Happy knew everybody's business and could tell you exactly what was happening in the hood. He had a good heart, so I kept him in my hood circle and used to look out for him with clothes and food all the time.

million times and I am kinda mad at her. Had she not come to the Mill, I would have kicked it with Deuce more than that one time. I know I can't change that, but I thought I'd put that out there because that's how I felt.

Once it's down in my entry and outta my head, hopefully that's the end of that thought or those feelings. I ain't feeling too in the Spirit right now cause I just thought about something else negative. I got a tooth rotting in my mouth and the blood is causing my spit to taste nasty. I have no insurance, so I am not sure how I am going to handle this. Mrs. Hilling gave me a number to an organization that does charity work, so I think I am going to call them and try to setup an appointment.

Well I'm going to let my brain rest. I'm afraid if I keep typing I'm going to get worse, so I'm going to go away, check some emails, search for God's blessings, do some work and just try to take my mind off the negative aspect of the things that have happened today.

3:18 p.m. 8/6/04 The School of Graduate Studies

I have been doing everything I can to stay positive and not forget about Deuce but keep my mind off of the negativity surrounding the situation. Man, I'm going to miss him a whole lot. I ain't gon' have nobody to kick it wit when I go back to the Mill and nobody to tell me what's been happening in the hood while I am away at school. Man, I'm going to miss slick Deuce.

On a positive note, I finally received the pictures that we took in Milwaukee of Missy and the family, and they ain't that bad. Charlene and Tiny are growing up and so is CJ. I'm starting to feel like an old man. That's why it's important that I redeem the time. I finally made a CD with Jodeci on it. I'll probably go home and pop that in and take a nice long nap cause I ain't too enthused to do much of anything. I called the clinic for people with no insurance and I have an appointment on Wednesday. It ain't for no STDs or nothing like that either, trout.[6] It's just to be going since it's free. I actually thought they offered dental services too, but since they don't that means I still gotta work on taking care of that. Still no word from Lala or ESPN. Doesn't look like I'll be going anywhere this weekend, but I'm not worried about it. Man, I really don't feel like doing nothing. I am going to try playing Live and doing something so I don't dwell on it, but I must say I am extremely hurt.

---

6 A Bingham family word that is short for trout-mouth nigga. It's a term used in jest to degrade someone. To be a trout mouth means to have jacked up teeth and bad breath. My family used it in jest a lot during this time. For example, if you don't get your trout-mouth off the phone jacking I'm gone call you out! Jacking means to exaggerate or basically be lying to make yourself look and feel good.

11:53 p.m. 8/6/04 Morgan View Lab
Where should I start? After work I just felt like a change so after putting up my things from work and unpacking my bag, I walked to the nearest barbershop which is right up the street to get my hair cut. I just couldn't shake this horrible feeling in the pit of my stomach, so I decided to do something drastic instead of trying to smoke away the pain or something crazy like that. After I got my hair cut I looked like a new man, yet I still felt the same on the inside—sick to my stomach and wishing I could escape the pain of knowing that my mans is gone.

On my way walking back to the room, I ran into Collins, the maintenance man. We had a nice lil chat about life and he gave me the scoop on one of the girls around the way. He's tricked on her and her friend on some real ish thinking they was gone recognize the real, but they ain't there yet. Now they think they pimped him and trying to play him like a lame. I figured it was something going on cause I can see she has newfound confidence. It was a nice distracting conversation. Hearing someone else's problems took my mind off Deuce or at least pushed it to the back for a while.

When I got to the room, I put all the recent trades in on NBA Live, saved that, then I headed to Herb's house in search of some competition but to no avail. It wasn't nothing going on over there but a bunch of smoking, so I got outta there but not before I grabbed a 22oz of Smirnoff Ice. I feel bad about buying it now and I felt bad about getting it then. I really didn't want it, but I was just sitting there bored and everybody else was drinking and watching Herb play the game. Going to get the drink was a reason for me to leave and try to find somewhere else to escape. I called Randy, but he was going to the Usher concert like just about every other female that I know. I called Santana and he was drinking, but at least I could find some kind of meaningful conversation there, so I went back and hollered at Herb them.

Now that I look back, I think I was sad and feeling down and sick to my stomach because of the responsibility that Deuce's death left on my shoulders. I got to make sure all my associates, friends and fam know that I am saved and that they need some insurance too cause one day you here and then you are gone.

Violet was sweating me when I made it back to the crib. She saw my hair was cut and literally chased me up the stairs trying to see. We ended up going out to eat at the Cheesecake Factory and that was a nice experience cause we had a nice conversation there, actually several nice conversations. Before they seated us, we walked the pier. I believe if Violet was hot and we did the things we do, I probably would be in love. But I'm not, so don't get it twisted. While eating, I got two calls from Nia, but I didn't feel like answering.

I called her back on the way back, and she said she went to church and they just so happened to be showing a video on abortion and she was sick to her stomach and felt like crying. She continued to tell me that she didn't trust herself to make the right decision and she was sure she would screw up. I just sat in silence because reverse psychology (I know that's cold) might have backfired, so I didn't say anything except I support you in whatever you do and I think you are going to make the right decision. I told her I believe in her and that nothing but good would come from this. After getting off the phone, I knew I shouldn't have called her back cause it was right back to feeling low and depressed.

Side note, Issa[7] replied to an email I sent her today talking bout she called me when I was here and I never called her back. Well darnit I'm human

---

[7] Issa grew up across the street from me in Milwaukee and was a few years older. Her little brother and I were very good friends that practically did everything together. She always treated me as something like a little brother, but I always admired her and thought she would ultimately be my wife when I was younger.

and I do forget sometimes. Today has been a day to say the least. I'm outta here. Oh yeah, Rick James died today too.

8

CONVO WITH VICK

5:34 p.m. 8/7/04 The Morgan View Lab

Today has been a day of business and relaxing. I did some cleaning up around the house and washed three loads of my clothes that had been piled up in the corner since I got back from the Mill. I woke up this morning at about 10:30 which is unusual for me on Saturday cause my nights used to be so rough. Anyway, I hopped out of bed on a mission to get something done today, redeem the time. So I threw on some clothes and went grocery shopping. I stocked up so I wouldn't have to spend so much money on fast food this month. I have been lazy as far as cooking goes and I got a feeling my pockets are about to start feeling it. This was my last big paycheck of the year. From here on out, I get a measly 1000 dollars to live off of for the month. While I was out grocery shopping, I stopped at the ATM to pull out my rent money. Sprint cut my phone off. I knew it had to be something though cause I didn't get not one call all day. I gotta get my phone on fast, just in case ESPN is trying to call. That would be disastrous, so I gotta go and pay this right away cause I got some cash on me. I'll holla later.

7:34 p.m. 8/7/04 The Morgan View Lab
Well I am back online as far as my phone is concerned. They received my payment of 80 dollars last week, but they cut my phone off cause they said I went over my minutes. How that happened, I don't know. I had to pay 40 dollars to get my phone back on—money that I really didn't have must I add. I had to get my phone on cause I don't want ESPN's HR department to have any excuse. I've given it to the Lord, so I ain't tripping. I also was lonely without my celly, cause today just seemed extra long without anybody annoying me. How ironic is that? I guess I'm just used to it.

I really just been chilling today, staying out of trouble, no urges to smoke or do anything wild. I have been listening to my music though. I don't know what it is. Maybe I just needed to feel closer to home or remember the good ol' days or at least days where I was doing better than I am now. I know I am about to hit a financial storm, going back to that 1000 dollars a month. Hopefully now that I'm not smoking I'll be able to find a side hustle so I can make some extra cash to get me through the month.

I gotta call home, Lala, Missy, Sheila, wanna call Issa, Violet, and last but not least Quin. Quin probably gone cuss me out cause I ain't answered her calls the past few days. I'm scared to call Nia, but something telling me I better call her before she call me trying to read and gauge me and see what my response gone be. I'm not sure if I really wanna hear her cause she be depressing a nigga wit all that baby talk cause she's not being positive. I mean I know it's hard to be positive, but I'm still skeptical about her really being serious about the whole situation. I don't know if she trying to see what kind of man I am or what.

I miss the Mill and I am not feeling content. I need to pray, study and hear some of His word. I need you, Jesus. I don't wanna be ungrateful, but today I have felt really needy. Like if I got some new kicks, a new outfit and maybe a new whip everything would be alright... or at least that's how I feel. I miss my nigga Deuce and I miss the Mill, and I definitely miss my truck. I ask God to humble me before I came out here and He did, cause had I had my truck, no one in Bmore would be able to tell me nothing. I would just hop in my truck and ride around and listen to my music to change my mood. I was listening to different CDs earlier to change my mood and they did temporarily.

1:47 p.m. 8/8/04 The Morgan View Lab

Today is Sunday and it felt good to go into the Lord's house and worship today. When I woke up this morning, I got a call from Vick. We had a man-to-man conversation about his current state and the state of those in our family. I redeemed the time and spoke to him about our Father God. I told him that I love him and I didn't want to see him leave this earth without the proper insurance and setting his business in order.

Last night I spoke with NeNe and she said Deuce's killing was all over the news. She seems to think Cardi had something to do with it also. I love Cardi, but from what I am hearing from other folks, the story just doesn't add up. It puts me in the mind of Tupac and Suge being in the car and Suge not getting hit. Something just ain't right. I've been told it doesn't even seem like Cardi is mourning. I spoke with Charlene yesterday about what's going on and she said that the next door neighbor saw everything and that she said when things die down she would tell Charlene the full story. It hurts my heart to even think Cardi had something to do with this. I knew she was cold, but I ain't sure if she that cold. Vick and everybody else seems to think she is. If she is, I don't see or even know what Deuce could have done to make her take her son's surrogate father away. Fat Mack loved Deuce just as much as me, if not more. He's going to be devastated by this for the rest of his life. It takes a real strong man to come in and raise someone else's son. That's what I told Vick this morning and he agreed with me.

Anyway, Charlene told me that when Deuce saw the pistol, he started backing up in the streets in front of a car and said, "Man, I didn't do nothing!" That scene played in my mind over and over last night. I could see Deuce's face and everything, and I felt his pain. He was just getting his life right. For some reason I just didn't see Cardi in my dreams though. She was nowhere in the picture. People might say Deuce was caught slipping, but I don't see it that way cause he wasn't wrong. That's why from what I've been told, he didn't run. He probably thought them cats had the wrong nigga. Man, it hurts.

Back to church, the same preacher who preached last Sunday preached this Sunday so I really didn't get fed again, so I am going back tonight cause Bro. Dashings is preaching at 5:30. There was good singing this morning though. We sung "Hard Fighting Soldier," "Home of the Soul," and "Sing and Be Happy" to name a few. Last night the *Five Heartbeats* came on and Eddie Cain tore it up! I love that movie now. It reminds me of Missy, but it also just makes my heart feel good to see brothers come together and stick with each other for a common goal. I guess I like it so much cause I wish I had true friends coming up like they were in the movie, for the most part. I don't think me and all my homies gone be able to meet up later in life though cause the majority are either going to be dead or too broke to do anything, and that's for real.

I went down front and asked the church to pray for me and the family because Deuce was taken from us. Mom said that Deuce's family is fighting already over Deuce's things and that's sad. I spoke with Charlene about it yesterday cause I wanted to know what Cardi was going to do with Deuce's car. Charlene said she was going to sell it. My thing was if you really loved and knew Deuce, he wouldn't have wanted his creation, what he worked so hard for, out there on the streets. If anything, he would've wanted me to have it. Although I know this is the truth deep in my heart, I don't wanna voice it because of all the drama surrounding the situation. I told Charlene to put a bug in Cardi's ear, but I doubt that works cause Cardi is a greedy so and so, and she probably will sell it to the highest bidder. Oh well, out of respect for Deuce I can't even say anything to her about it cause I see that as being disrespectful and coming at her sideways like the rest of them niggas that he used to deal with. I guess I'll have to leave that alone, but it hurts to even think Cardi is that shiesty. I don't know if I can even talk to her straight up anymore, but like Charlene said: the truth shall come to the light.

7:41 p.m. 8/8/04 The Morgan View Lab

Boy, I am feeling so much better! I had a nap and I actually fell asleep pretty easy. I don't remember what I dreamed about, but I did wake up in time for church. Brother Dashings tore it up! It was much better than this morning's sermon. He was on fire! He talked about the exceedingly sinfulness of sin and how it separates us from God. He talked about how deceptive it is and how the pleasures of sin only last a short while, long enough to separate you and having you stand a guilty distance from God. When I say he tore it up, I mean he tore it up. He talked about how sin is barely used in the English language today. He talked about how homosexuality is called being gay, fornication is called having sex, adultery is called having an affair, and he showed many more examples of how in this sinful world today, sin is downplayed dramatically through the use of language.

On the way home from church Charlene called and told me Sonia and Kevin was fighting in front of the house. Kevin is my other ace, but he's moved to Minnesota. Charlene said he busted out Sonia's car window but didn't tell her and had her all revved up to jump on Sonia if she came over the house. Charlene said that Sonia pulled up in the middle of the street, hopped out and said, "Charlene, this nigga done busted my window." So Charlene fell back and let them handle their business. Anyway, drama is everywhere at home and here for me. Vick hasn't called me back and I don't know if I should call him or just let him be.

Being in church felt good. If I didn't have to worry about gas I would go to Sunday evening worship all the time, but I don't think I would be able to make it to all the Sunday, Tuesday and Wednesday services if I went to all of them every week, so I have to pick and choose. Maybe that's something I can pray on, because I have the desire to be there, but circumstances (or at least it seems) would prevent me. Maybe that's just Satan? I am going to make an attempt to be there whenever the doors open, although I don't think I am going to go next Sunday. I am going to try to go to Nia's church so I can get an unofficial look at the family seeing as how she is undecided on what she wants to do. I think I am going to call Granny and some other folks, so I am going to end this entry. Hopefully, I will have something positive to say and will come back later on tonight. If not, God is still good cause I ain't smoked nothing in two (or is it three?) weeks. I ain't sure, but I know I am doing good and I am going to make it through this Deuce situation without smoking.

9

PULL OF SHERMAN MERMAN'S COATTAIL

9:07 a.m. 8/9/04 The School of Graduate Studies

Today started off good. I am grateful that God has spared me another day, even though I am not worthy and didn't do anything to deserve this day. Yesterday, after I got back from church, Loban and I rode to Randy house to get some boots and just holla at him for a minute. On the way there, on probably the busiest, fastest street in Baltimore, a young girl probably about 20-something was jaywalking across the street with a baby and a dude. She was holding the child's hand and just taking her time, and the light was green as grass. I had to be doing at least 70 mph and they saw me coming and did not speed up. The bad thing about it is she had the child on my side of the street. I saw the child, and that was the reason I slowed down. I almost came to a screeching halt. She hollered something at me as I drove past. I thought hard about going back and asking her if her life was that bad that she would do something that bad and suicidal. She put the child's life at risk and I didn't see nothing cool or hard about that cause this ain't no normal street. It ain't no lawsuit if you get hit on this street, cause at the speeds the street permits you dead. Ain't no broke legs or arms or nothing like that. You flying in the air and you is finished. Loban went to pleading with me like man that's foolishness man don't pay no attention, and I thought about it and pulled off. I let it slide, but now that I think about it I shouldn't have let that slide.

Anyway, that was on my mind. We also went to Herb's house last night and was just chilling, talking to some chicks from Baltimore County that thought they was pimps. That was interesting. After we walked back, I went to see one of my friends with benefits. She's still on her hiatus and I told her that's cool. Without the sex, she's really not that interesting though. Sad to say but true. Oh, Tika[8] and I had a very interesting conversation last night at Herb's house. She called me talking slick and got Mr.GoodGame to come out for a minute, but after he put her in line and let her know he was the smoothest, fastest slick talker, she kind of eased up. Then she felt put in her place, so she came at me again and I had to hang

---

[8] Tika didn't play a large role in my life. Off and on, she was someone I'd call for an occasional hookup.

up on her cause I didn't want to be cussing and all out of character so I let that conversation go. She really knows how to bring him out and I am trying to put him on the shelf. I told her that, but she doesn't believe me. I've told her that before, so she is one of them I will have to just show.

That brings me to today, and now you see why it is a blessing for me to be given another day. Even though I went to church yesterday morning and evening, I really didn't do anything to glorify the Lord. I didn't smoke anything, but I gotta get myself together and get the mote out of my eye before I try to tell anybody about what's in their eye.

Mom called me this morning, we talked about Deuce, and she told me what she knows. I told her that there was something shiesty about what happened and she just thinks that whole lifestyle is shady and I agree with her, but I don't think she really know what I mean. I didn't want to tell her that I think her adopted daughter, Cardi, may have had something to do with it. We talked about Vick and Kevin's lil incident yesterday.

I also went online and found a dentist, so I'm going to check and see how much a tooth extraction costs and setup an appointment if it ain't too much. Still no word from ESPN or Lala. Oh yeah, I also talked to Sheila last night and that fool answered the phone talking bout "Holla!" That was hilarious! She has got too much time on her hands, cause she is truly getting ghetto and it is so funny cause she reminds me of my mom when she tries to get ghetto cause it really doesn't agree with her at all. It's like she is so peculiar and godly that when she tries to be worldly it is so funny cause she can't, which is great in my eyes!

Well today is starting real well. Dr. Mavis Bicks just walked in on me and asked if I was going for a job interview because of my haircut and said she would give me a glowing reference if I needed it and I didn't even have to ask! Now time for the message for the day.

Reclaim Your Power's inspirational theme is Be a mentor. I think that I will be carrying out that duty real soon. I'm trying to get nephew sent out here to me and I am going to try my best to be an example to the youth in the church. I have been going to the youth group meetings for the adults after church and they have an event this weekend. I figure that will be my introduction to most of the kids. I see the way they eye me up and down and what I got on when I come to church on Tuesday and Wednesday nights, so I will use that to my advantage. I am going to go fresh to death on Friday cause Saturday I will probably be with Nia.

Speaking of which, I called her last night and just let her know I was thinking about her and am here for her. I am currently talking to Charlene through the IM service and she's telling me about how Sonia called the house and apologized last night. I knew Sonia was good folks. Charlene said that Kandi, one of his baby mamas, called the house like 10 times last night cause Kevin didn't come to see the kids. Something done happened to my nigga in Minnesota cause that ain't the Kevin I know.

Back to the mentoring, I figure if I come fresh to death as usual, one of the kids may see me as cool and want to figure out what I'm doing with my life and that will give me a chance to glorify God and drop some jewels on 'em. Steve Mandy was a mentor in my life and I love him for it. He was just cool and supported me in the things I tried to do and I will never forget him. It felt good to talk to him the other day, and I learned to be humble from him cause he was such a humble man although he was living a good life. Deuce was a mentor, for a while . . . .

The scripture of the day reads: *It is done. I am Alpha and Omega, the beginning and the end. I will give unto him that is athirst of the fountain of the water of life freely. He that overcometh shall inherit all things; and I will be his God, and he shall be my son* (Revelation 21: 6-7). This verse serves as inspiration to overcome this flesh and the worldly sins associated with the flesh to inherit everlasting life. It states that God is the alpha and omega and that He is a loving God and can be found by those who are truly seeking. I have to remember that these earthly things are going to be here when I am dead and gone, so my real goal should be to reach heaven and preserve my soul before it is too late. Oh yeah, my big toenail on my left foot fell off today, and Mom seems to think that it is diabetes so I gots to be real careful.

3:38 p.m. 8/9/04 The Morgan View Lab
Like Mase, guess who's back? For lunch I went home and prepared myself two Hot Pockets. I also received some paperwork from the Shepherd's Clinic, so I should finally get an opportunity to get a checkup. I've been listening since I got back to the Hot 97 interview with Mase, and it's funny cause people are hating on him cause he's trying to do the right thing. There was not one positive phone-in for him, all were hypocritical judges trying to prove how phony he was. But he handled them well cause he was in the Spirit and prepared for all the hate and fielded the questions real well.

It was almost like the Pharisees and Sadducees coming at Jesus. He answered all the questions out of love. It was as if they were mad he was trying to bring righteousness to the industry, cause many of them were so mad and accusing that they didn't even want to let him speak. They were just throwing mud, but it was like Mase has come to a deeper understanding because Cam and Jim Jones, two of his old associates, came at him and basically threatened him, but he has God's confidence. He is a strong brother and he is on a mission by himself. He is healed and delivered in Jesus's name.

9:03 a.m. 8/10/04 The School of Graduate Studies

A lot has transpired since we last spoke, so I am going to do my best to fill you in. Let's backtrack to yesterday. When I got off work, Violet and I walked back to the crib together and changed clothes cause I was actually dressed yesterday in a casual yet slick Perry Ellis Portfolio ensemble. We went to an organic grocery store and on the way back we stopped at Godfrey's and got some Damien wings. Man, I love their wings! We ate the wings in my room and watched Badder Santa with Billy Bob Thorton, and that cracker is something else in that movie! Just as we were finishing up the wings, I hear a knock at the door and it's Chasity and Sandra, the new tenant in the building. They stopped by for a minute and chitchatted with Violet and me. I keep forgetting, but I have to take those pictures down in my room[9] because although they add flavor, it doesn't help in God's ministry and they keep me lusting so I have to remember to take those pictures down definitely before the nephews get here. Anyway, while they were all there it dawned on me that I had to get a money order so I left them in my room and mashed to the gas station. When I got back, Violet was still chilling but said Sandra was sleepy so Chasity left with her. Good riddance. So Violet and I got comfortable in the bed. No hanky panky, she and I are just comfortable like that and she finished watching the movie and I went to sleep. After the movie went off, she left and I called Sherman Merman cause she called me while I was with Violet on the way headed to the store, and I had to snap on her cause she was asking me all kinds of questions that she shouldn't have been asking me.

Sherman Merman is one of the first females here that I took to and that took to me. When I

---

[9] I had a subscription to KING magazine, a Black man's magazine, so I had all of the Eye Candy centerfold model foldouts on my bedroom wall, including Ki Toy Johnson, Melyssa Ford, Esther Baxter, Trina, Rosa Costa and others. While the models were not fully nude, the outfits were skimpy and the poses suggestive.

first met her, she asked what a pimp was and I told her I would show her and the rest has been history. So I put P on it when I had marinated it and this nigga really ain't got no G, so she call herself trying to hide they business from me. She wasn't bright enough to know I put P on and he tells me everything like a lil B.I.

Sherman Merman gave me money, food, head and shoulders[10] and her car whenever I wanted. She was truly a blessing cause when I needed groceries or personal hygiene items, she always bought me what I needed. I abused it though and one day she gave me her car and I went out, got high and ignored her phone calls. When I got back, she got the police to come with her to my house so she could get her keys. I've had to exercise the pimp hand on her cause she pushed me too far and basically forced me to put my hands on her cause she put her hands on me first while I was driving.

Anyway, I went down there and talked to her cause she kept calling me asking me when I was coming. So I get down there and she still lying to me in my face about what she does in her private time, so I let it go for a minute and then she let it slip that Loban borrowed a can of my tuna and

---

10 Slang term for "oral sex"

came to her to replace it instead of asking me for some food cause he hungry and refuse to ask his pops for money. So now I'm hot cause there is no way I should be hearing this from her. I like to think that Loban and I have a real relationship where if he really hungry he can ask for some of my food, not think he has to sneak and eat it and replace it without me knowing. Because she didn't want me to say nothing, she performed some mouth and lip service to soothe me. Like an idiot, still weak in that area, I let her do it and then ended up taking a quickie cause I was already aroused. After that, she starts telling me why she really hasn't messed with me this summer, saying it's because I'm too busy following up behind P and company and I ain't never got time for her. That triggered me again and I had to set the record straight that she got it twisted and that those niggaz follow up behind me.

Once I established my dominance she started singing like a bird and spilled the beans on how she has been agonizing over how she was going to tell me that she fooled around with P, his roommate, and how she had been buying Loban food cause he was basically begging her to. After that crying testimony I sat her down and let her know that I had been known all of these things. I just wasn't going to come out and expose my whole hand cause that ain't what I do. She started seeing that the rest are carbon copies and new to this while yours truly is true to this. She felt a whole lot better knowing she didn't have to lie to me.

I shouldn't have had sex with her and that broke my streak because it's been a while. I say it started off good cause I actually felt bad about it and it was on my conscience so before I even set foot out the bed I laid there and talked to God about the situation and asked for forgiveness because I was thinking all kinds of thoughts that made me fear God's wrath. I really didn't enjoy it and after hearing Sunday evening's service I should have known better. I should have been stronger. God is working on me though and I count it all joy still. Soon, Lord's will, I will be able to push the lustful thoughts out of my mind like He helped me push the thoughts about smoking out my mind. God is good cause I haven't smoked yet and I feel great and haven't really been depressed a whole lot or going through withdrawal. I have been in so many storms and He has brought me through them all, so I always had faith that one day He would bring me through. I just didn't know when. Now that you are caught up, I am going to check some emails and get the inspirational message for the day.

10

BACK TO THE ILL MILL WITH SHEILA

10:19 a.m. 8/12/04 The School of Graduate Studies

Boy, Satan is really trying to get at me. It took this long for me to get back atcha cause I was straying to be perfectly honest, looking at some stuff I know I shouldn't have been on the internet—porn on a dating website that someone sent me an invitation to. I know I ain't supposed to be looking at that stuff and I was telling myself that as I was checking out the different young ladies' profiles, but it took me this long to pull away. O wretched body and mind of mine. I just pray that the Lord doesn't run out of mercy for me cause sometimes, as far as my sexual nature goes, I can really be pathetic. I gotta get stronger and I pray and ask God to help me with that. I have faith that He is going to pull me through. I just pray that it ain't too late and the effects aren't too devastating. I know that one day He is going to take the lustfulness out of my heart like He's taken the desire to smoke from me. I think this is the longest I have gone without smoking anything for about 5 years. Yeah, I'm proud of myself and I thank God for making it this easy and giving me a way out.

The inspirational theme for the day is faith (how ironic is this?). Faith is leaning not unto thine own understanding. When I left the crib this morning, that's what Bro. Gains was preaching about on the tape. Even through these times that may look perilous and the financial burdens which are about to hit, I am going to keep my head up and know that God is going to make it alright. The exercise asks what experience has made me uncertain or doubtful. Well I must say that I tend to get down on myself for not trusting in the Lord and having faith when I know He's brought me through so many storms.

Lately I have had so many different financial obligations that it looks like I'm not going to be able to meet. I've been doubtful and uncertain about it, which has caused my faith to waver and dampened my spirit. It asks am I willing to release them and have faith, and the answer is yes. I am so glad that I have this book cause this message definitely hits home today. I am so blessed that sometimes I forget. When He brings me through a storm, I forget to thank him, so right now I am going to take the time out to say "Thank you, God! You truly are a magnificent God! Thank you for loving me more than I love myself and for having mercy upon my soul because I am not worthy! I release my worries to you and I let go. I know that you will handle things in a timely manner according to your will. Help me not to worry or stress or even give thought to these things, and when I do please plant your seed and give me a word to block out the evil thoughts." Boy, that felt great. I needed it for sure. That's how I will release it.

The scripture for the day is: *And these signs shall follow them that believe; In my name shall they cast out devils; they shall speak with new tongues; They shall take up serpents; and if they drink any deadly thing, it shall not hurt them; they shall lay hands on the sick, and they shall recover* (Mark 16:17-18). This verse is dealing with Jesus before he ascended into the Heavens. The verses before this He was giving them His final commandments and told them to go in the world and teach all nations and preach the gospel and He that believeth and is baptized shall be saved. That's where these verses come in. I'm not sure how I would apply this, but I will think about it and get back to you.

I spoke with Missy and I now have an itinerary printed out, so I feel so much better. I will holla later. The next time we speak I'm probably going to be in the Mill.

3:40 p.m. 8/14/04 My Crib in the Mill

I didn't leave Baltimore until like 8:00 which is an hour later than I was supposed to leave. Ironically, Hurricane Charley delayed my plane for an hour therefore throwing off Sheila's, my ride, schedule. Well I was blessed to make it to the Chi safely. God is good and it was even a decent flight—no layover and I got to pick my seat cause I rode Southwest and they are supposed to be one of the better airlines nowadays. Well I arrived in Midway and got my bags and went outside to wait on Sheila. While I was waiting, I was entertained by the traffic controllers at the airport. Boy, they was something serious! They wasn't letting anybody slide. You had to be picked up at the curb and you better had hurried up and put your bags in the car and get ghost. It was hilarious. Some white couples were trying to hug before they put their bags in the trunk and the traffic controller would come right behind them and blow the whistle.

When I hopped in the car, Sheila was looking great! She was kind of surprised that I didn't get a hug, but when I hopped in I was concerned about keeping it moving, because I had been out there with the traffic controllers so long that I knew they was gone get ugly wit a black man. Sheila and I went and got some gas and looked at pictures. We sat there and caught up on old times and tried to decide what we were going to do first. We decided not to rush back to the Mill and to ride around Chi-town like we own it instead. We ended up riding around downtown going to Navy Pier. Downtown Chi-town is really romantic and I didn't have to say much to set any type of mood. When we went to Navy Pier we had so much fun! When we got there it was like 10:45 p.m. and it closed at 12. It was like we had the park to ourselves.

We snuck in a Fun House Maze and we ended up running out the first time because we went down a dark tunnel and they had some airbursts we didn't know about and scared the crap out of us. We decided to man up and run back in, and I'm glad we did cause it was really fun. After we left the Fun House, we walked through the park and just held each other on some real romantic type ish. We also went to Bubba Gump's Shrimp house and ate good! I like that place a lot and will have to visit it again on Sheila's expense next time I frequent the Chi. After we left there we stopped in the greenhouse and cuddled and kissed with very little talking and more hugging and kissing.

This is where Sheila got her first kissing lesson. When we first started to kiss, she tried to shove her tongue down my throat like she was trying to choke me. I had to let her know that I wasn't going anywhere and I wasn't in a rush so we stayed until we got it right. We stayed until both of us were hot and bothered, then we rode around some more and made up our mind on what we were going to do. We went back to her modest place. Syke! I'm being facetious, because I was tricked! Sheila is living good! She stay in downtown Chi in a high rise on the 13th floor with a skyline view overlooking the Chi with the Sears Tower included. It is sooo romantic in her apartment that Mr. Thang got hard soon as I seen the view. Seriously!

We were there longer than expected and her mom saved the day, cause we were getting even more hot and bothered with each other when her mom called and said to meet her at the Sears Tower at 1:15 p.m. Of course, we were late. I didn't want to get her in trouble and I didn't wanna meet Moms for the first time on bad terms, so she dropped me off around the corner and went and dropped her keys off to her mom. After that we headed to the Mill, and I was drop dead tired cause I had been up since 7 a.m. It felt like I lost an hour coming back to the Mill on the plane, so I had serious jetlag. I tried to be a soldier for Sheila, but it was a serious struggle and I sounded like a complete fool cause she was asking me questions and I was all off my circle. I was so tired that I would go deep to sleep and wake back up like 10 seconds later like *What did you ask me?*

We made it back to the Mill at about 2:30 and Aunt Fanny let us in the house. Friday morning, we went to the funeral. Sheila was wonderful and I don't know anyone like her. I want to spoil her with all that I can give. She is beyond anything that I could ever hope for. She's right when she says that I'm not upfront with everything. Sometimes I can be a little deceptive or misleading, but I mean well. Sometimes people don't need to know everything and what they don't know won't hurt them. If people ask though I'd tell the truth, therefore I can't be considered a liar. Sheila started these last couple of lines and I am finishing them. I hope she feels really special because she is the only person who has had some kind of input into my story. Anyway, I really did appreciate her being at the funeral because I know I wouldn't want to spend my free time at a funeral unless I really loved that person. Sheila is messing with me so I will continue this later.

11

SEE YOU AT THE CROSSROADS

9:14 a.m. 8/16/04 The School of Graduate Studies

At the funeral, Deuce packed the house! It was so many fine women in there it didn't make no sense, and you know they was dressed to the nines, from head to toe. During the funeral procession to the gravesite, there was over 160 cars and the procession was deep and filled with ballers. It was almost like a car show or a car parade. Of course you had your whooptis[11] and trappers,[12] but it was some slick cars and plenty niggaz riding on rims and spinners. As we were driving through the streets, people were standing outside and coming out of the barbershops and corner stores just to watch us pass.

After the procession Sheila and I went home to change clothes then we hit 27th. I could tell she

---

[11] A "whoopti" in Milwaukee slang is known as a beat-up, worn-out car. Typically, these cars had visible rust, were missing a visible part like a bumper, side mirror, door handle or some other defect like a trunk that was taped down or a very loud engine. Other names used were beater or jalopy.

[12] A "trapper" in Milwaukee slang is a whoopti with a special defect that could get you killed or captured by the police if you ever needed to make a quick getaway. These were typically driven by folks selling drugs or doing other illegal activities, and the car typically had a door that could only be unlocked or opened a certain way or a door that just didn't open.

wasn't all that comfortable cause Cardi's brother was slobbering over her telling her she look like Nia Long. I found it funny and told her about his con-man background after we left. Later on, I believe we went and got some ice cream or something. It's not fresh on my mind cause we did so much while I was there. We went to Red Lobster with Judy, a family friend, and clowned. I mean we was acting like the Bundys or something. The manager ended up taking Sheila and my meal off the bill, so we ate good for free. We then proceeded to Roberts on 68th and Capitol where Judy and I turned the music up in the parking lot and two-stepped to Keith Sweat and I was bugging to Young Buck's "Let Me In."

After that we went to the crib and Sheila and I spent some much-needed quality time together. She picked up on the kissing pretty quick and we just explored each other for a while before going to bed. Saturday morning Mom and the family went to Perkins and left me and Sheila, so we went to Ja'Stacy's and ate. We were in the restaurant singing along with the music which was Mary J Blige's *Share My World* CD. After that she and I went to the crib and just lounged and cuddled. We tracked my mom them down and found out they went to State Fair, so we chilled for a while then Sheila dropped me off on 27th and she went to get her car washed. I spent some quality time with the nephews and got a PS2 joystick finally. Deuce had them lil niggaz so spoiled, they had eight joysticks just laying around.

While on 27th I put a bug in Judy's daughter's ear cause she came outside with what look like some sleepwear pants, but you could see her booty through them and she really got it all from her mama. I actually had to grab it and it was soft as a pillow. She told me she is single now, so I know the next time I go home it's on and popping. Although her eyes and her body was saying yes, she kept saying no. I wasn't gone beg, so I had to leave her alone. I rode with Ty and one of his other cousins to the t-shirt shop and placed my order for a RIP t-shirt. I ended up getting the player's deal on my t-shirt too! That's a whole 'nother story though.

When I got back on 27th, I let Fat Mack ride his bike to my house. Mom them was there and were headed back to State Fair. Oh and a very important thing to remember is that I forgot to bring my charger on this trip, so I was basically out of touch with everyone except Sheila. There was no creeping for me, but I was actually satisfied cause I didn't know what I was missing seeing as how my celly was out of commission.

Sheila ain't got no radio in her car, so we had to sing on the way to the Chi and believe me my nerves were bad cause the roads were packed and folks really can't drive. I was woosahing the whole way there. When we got close to Chi, Sheila pulled out a CD player with some headphones and we listened to Lauryn Hill. We were the definition of HOTGHETTOMESS.COM. I was swerving in and out of traffic dipping with my head leaning toward the inside of the car with one ear piece in my ear sharing the other with Sheila. How you like that?! When I got to the airport, two cuties at the check-in counter told me that my flight was delayed and wasn't departing until 11:30, even though it was only 8:30. I went to my gate to confirm the departure time then I called Sheila. She came and scooped me and we went to Arby's and talked. The main topic was why she was hiding me from her family. I believe she is either ashamed of me or of her family. What she was telling me, I ain't feeling.

*

You just followed me back to Milwaukee and gained more insight into the environment and people that helped to shape me. Deuce was one of those people who had a true impact on my life and his murder helped push me closer to my purpose.

Despite how much of a jerk I may have seemed in my entries in describing people, I always treated people with respect regardless of who you were. Or at least I tried. I learned from Deuce's murder that one of the best gifts, if not the best gift, to give someone is not respect but to help them understand the importance of making sure their soul is saved.

The person who shaped me the most was my mom. She prepared me for my walk by instilling the word of God in me and my siblings. For example, growing up when my siblings and I got in trouble, she would sit us all down and make us read an appropriate scripture before "whooping" us. I would say beating, which we called it during the time, but this is a new age and it doesn't feel right telling someone to beat their kids. However, the Bible does command parents to discipline their child with a rod, so I believe in corporal punishment. She also made sure I knew the teachings of the book of Proverbs, was exposed to all types of leadership activities, knew how to use my hands, and most importantly, she taught me how to think.

For the most part of my life, my mom was a single mom even though she remained married to my father. Since my father was not the best role model, she also did her best to make sure I was around good male role models. Grandpa Hill was one of these individuals. He was one of the elder members of my church at Hampton Avenue Church of Christ. He would pick me up often on the weekends and spend time with me doing various activities. He and his wife Grandma Hill were a big inspiration and showed me how a man should conduct himself and how a husband and wife should treat each other. You will hear about Grandma Hill later.

I was also shaped by the world. Ironically, before I went to Morgan State, while working at the TV station as an engineer, I started reading all kinds of urban novels by Zane, Eric Jerome Dickey and Donald Goines. I had a union engineering job, so I wasn't allowed to do anything else on my shift. One day, one of the video editors had one on their desk that they had just finished and allowed me to read it, and that was my introduction to this type of literature.

I also read Iceberg Slim's *Pimp*. I point out to people who've read it that in *Pimp*, Iceberg got his game while he was in Milwaukee before he went to Chicago. It's just something about Milwaukee that forces you to step up your mental game and level up yourself, situational awareness and emotional intelligence, or you will either end up dead or in prison.

The Death of Mr. GoodGame

I recently saw a CNN special on Milwaukee that stated it was statistically the worst place for African-American males. When I tell people I'm from Milwaukee, they typically ask if there are any black folks there and I almost always reply that there are plenty of niggas there. I mean that in the truest sense of the word: ignorant individuals.[13] I am truly blessed to have made it out of that place. Milwaukee is like a prison for black folks because they have successfully confined most of the blacks to living below the poverty line to the north side. The rest of Wisconsin is farms and prisons. Madison is different because it is a college town due to the University of Wisconsin. Most of the black people that I know that moved to Madison are uppity blacks that have become accustomed to living and dealing with racism and would rather tolerate racism than deal with their own people. I'm glad my mom refused to put us in that environment, and I really think it has helped me to better relate to my people who are less for-

---

13 There has been much debate over the past couple of years over African American's use of the word. Generally, there are two schools of thought regarding its use in our community. One school of thought says we should never use that word to refer to other African Americans. My mom falls into this school. The other school of thought believes we have taken the word back and it can be used as a term of endearment. I fall in this latter category. I use it all the time to refer to those in my close circle. For example, I will say "what's up my nigga" or "that's my nigga." In this instance, I am not using it as a term of endearment. Like Chris Rock, I love my black people, but sometimes I can't stand niggas.

tunate and can't seem to find a way out of their mental prisons. One of the reasons I am sharing my memoir is to inspire those who also come from a place of hopelessness and despair to show them that through education they can make it out too!

I have always contended that our educational system in America is all screwed up and needs to be fixed. I still have my report cards from elementary and middle school, and just about all of my teachers would give me the "Great Student" mark then would add "Talks too much in class." Teachers tried to label me with ADHD and put me in special ed classes with kids who had learning disabilities and behavior problems, but my mom always fought against that. Once you are in those classes, you eventually are put in a feeder school which we called "alternative." This is where they sent kids with learning disabilities and behavioral issues; this was the pipeline to prison.

During elementary school, I would finish the simple and boring work the teachers assigned early then talk to my classmates. Some of my teachers preferred that I just sit and twiddle my thumbs quietly, but my mom fixed that! Eventually I was tested and put in "Gifted and Talented" classes, so I was spared from the school-to-prison pipeline that Milwaukee is notorious for. Why did I bring that up? I bring it up because I've also grown to feel the same about our standardized testing system. It is based on eugenics and rooted in racism. Do your own research on eugenics and you will be disgusted. It is important that we don't allow the American educational system and standardized testing system rooted in racism to define who we are are as a people or miseducate our children.

While getting my master of arts in teaching at Morgan State University, I saw firsthand just how screwed up our educational system is. The politics and not being able to teach my students what I knew they needed and the way I wanted to teach them to help them survive and thrive in life due to No Child Left Behind is partly why I left the profession. I suspect that there are many teachers leaving the profession for a similar reason today. Some of the teachers in predominantly African-American schools, like the 2011 movie *Bad Teacher* with Cameron Diaz, are only there for a check and could not care less about our kids. This is exactly why my wife and I sacrificed her quarter-million-dollar salary at a top law firm, Sullivan & Cromwell, to homeschool our children.

It may seem like I've gone on a tangent here, but it is important to note that it is critical that we make sure we educate our children so they can find and walk in their purpose. To some extent, at least for some, our educational system is nothing but a distraction that keeps you from fulfilling your purpose. I've seen our education system put the fire out, kill the creativity and confidence, and kill the soul of many a minority children. Watch the *Who Shot Malcolm X?* documentary on Netflix to hear how Malcom X's teacher tried to stop him from his purpose. Malcolm could've been a lawyer, but his teacher convinced him it wasn't a reasonable goal. However, she didn't stop him from finding his purpose as he still became an eloquent and renowned speaker, as history shows.

With that said, if I was my LSAT score and it was an accurate assessment of my potential, I wouldn't be where I'm at right now—an award-winning tech attorney. Thank God I got into Howard University School of Law! One of the best faith decisions I made! (HU! You Know! HUSL Gang forever!) If you want to succeed in the game of life, as I tell my mentees, one of the lessons I learned from this time period is to know thyself.

At this point, I had identified one of my strongholds as smoking and had committed to overcoming that mountain. However, you will see that I had more than one stronghold pulling on me; I also had an addiction to sex and the attention and admiration of women. While I was doing a good job dealing with not smoking, it led to me being overly confident that I had reached my mark. My sex addiction, which I had not fully committed to overcoming, became a trigger that caused me to stumble more and more. Throughout my journey, my sex addiction was a thorn in my side that kept me humble as you will see.

Self-control and self-awareness are tremendous assets in accomplishing your goals. To accomplish my goals, I had to build up some self-control and self-awareness to realize and recognize my triggers that knocked me off-balance. My pride in the form of Mr.GoodGame, an alter ego, got in my way. However, I realized that if you acknowledge God in all your ways, He will truly direct your path. That path may not be easy, but God is a great captain.

12

EMOTIONAL CONFESSION— MR. GOODGAME WINNING

8/17/04 The Morgan View Lab

Mrs. Hilling brought lunch from Godfrey's for the office. She gave me the keys to the Maxima and had me go get it. It felt pretty good to be riding in something halfway slick. Plus, I was getting looks from other chicks in whips cause I brought my Young Buck CD and was jamming. When I got back, Dr. Tailor had me doing an assignment for him or should I say redoing one. When it's time for letters of recommendation, I hope he remembers me this summer and my ability to produce. After work Violet followed me to Midas where I dropped off my truck so they can find out what's wrong with it. Lord's will it will be ready by Friday in time for my doctor's appointment; I'm also going to try and be a walk-in at the dentist.

I still had my Godfrey wings, so dinner was taken care of. Issa called me while I was eating, so I told her I would call her back in five minutes. That heffa didn't even answer. She's good for that and that's a big part of the reason we ain't hooked up yet, cause I don't deal with that. It's all good though cause if it's meant to be it'll pop off. Issa was my first crush and the first girl that I knew I liked. She used to play me though like I was too young or too much of a goody goody. She still tries to play me but not because she think I'm a goody goody but because she know I got girls and I ain't the shy lil boy that I used to be anymore.

I walked to the store while talking to Missy and got me some sporting waves, so I'm about to try to get to spinning before school officially starts. Missy said she will be getting a free scooter for school, so I am happy for her. I had messages from her and a few others. I forgot all about my buddy Jasmine when I went back home, but I know I ain't forgetting about all these folks during Christmas so it's all good. It's going to be a wonderful Christmas as long as I got some wheels.

The joystick that I brought from home works, so that's good. The Packers lost their first preseason game to the Seahawks last night. I had to get Loban this morning or actually leave a note for Loban about the shower cause he be taking showers and leaving the dirt in there. I would have told him straight up of course, but I don't ever see the nigga anymore. I'm probably going to call Sheila then go play a game and call it a night. I pray that the mechanic working on my car don't try to shiest me on the price. Oh yeah, I ain't smoked nothing, so I'm still good on my streak. Continue to pray for me and look out.

9:35 a.m. 8/18/04 The School of Graduate Studies

I have really been struggling with looking at porno on the internet. Satan has been on my table since I've been back and he has been trying to make me feel horrible because I know I shouldn't be looking at the stuff, but I don't turn away cause my eyes like what they see. Oh, this wretched body of mine! That sucks to want to do something and not be able to do it. I literally be trying to get off the sites, but I continue diving deeper and deeper cause I always see an image that my eyes feel like they just have to see. Lust is a mother for real! I've been doing great as far as not smoking is concerned. Now it's the porn and lustful thoughts that I have to escape, and I think God may actually be able to use me. I feel like Satan is mad and know he is losing his power over me because I've taken the pictures of the women down in my room and I feel a deep change coming. I just got to get away from these lustful thoughts, and the best way that I know how to do that is to pray and fill my mind up with God's word. That sounds really good, but it's easier said than done, especially for me, cause I just love women.

Last night I basically chilled, didn't get into any trouble. I spoke with Quin, Sheila, Mom and Nia. Mrs. Nia told me I wasn't her friend anymore and I can accept that cause I wasn't there for her and she is probably angry so I am just going to leave that situation alone and stop calling cause I was blessed to escape without a deeper commitment. Sheila is doing good. Oh, and I also spoke with Missy and found out her birthday is on September 27th, the same day that Tweety was born, so that is very significant and may explain why Mom is so compassionate about her. I now have newfound respect for her all over again, because I never knew Tweety's birthday and now I do because of her.

Everything else is slow motion. I think the mechanics didn't do a thorough job on my truck when I got it fixed, so I am going to call my dad and see what they could have screwed up so when they call me I can say that's y'all fault and y'all can't charge me for y'all not doing a complete and thorough job. Better yet, I know I should pray about it. I think that's what I am going to do—just take a break from work and pray.

The inspirational theme for the day is: Move, Mountain, Get Out of My Way! Fall down 7 times, stand up 8. I think that is the story of my life. I am always doing dumb stuff and falling down, stumbling or just falling from grace, and God always helps me to stand back up and continue on. God is good all the time and I thank Him for the present which He has given me, which is today. The exercise asks what mountains am I ready to move out of my way. I'm ready to remove these lustful thoughts. Lord, help me please, cause I can't do it on my own. I think I am going to make a prayer list right now of things I need to pray for when I take my break.

The scripture of the day: *But as many as received Him, to them gave He power to become the sons of God, even to them that believe on His name* (John 1:12). This applies to me and my life because I know I am a son of God although I don't always act like it I know there is a higher calling on my life because I have faith. I'm not sure exactly what God's plan is for me, but I do have faith that I am going to stop being ignorant one day and just totally submit to His will. Oh what a glorious day that will be! I just pray I wake up before it's everlasting too late. I believe in the confession I made on February 2, 1992 that Jesus Christ is the Son of

God and died on the cross for my sins. I still have problems in my life because I tend to forget the great sacrifice that He made and that is most likely cause I am just now becoming sober minded. I also don't always exhibit the behavior that should go with this confession because I'm not watchful and Satan tends to sneak up and slip into my thoughts from behind. I know He's given me power though, or He wouldn't have allowed me to make it this far.

I often dream about the effect I can have on so many souls if it's His will that I preach and come out of this sinful lifestyle like Paul. I feel that I could be such a powerful speaker because I've been through it and done it before like Mase. It won't be much that I can't see if I tune my spirit with God cause I already got book knowledge, common sense and street smarts. What a sermon that would be if I was only given a chance. I listen to different preachers preach. Some are good and some are not, and I wonder what it would be like if I was up there. Only thing is fear usually comes into my thoughts about what would happen if the congregation found out I was such a great sinner and had lustful thoughts. I know that's Satan cause God doesn't give us a spirit of fear, but I am just telling you how I often feel. I sure would have some testimonies!

An example of a sin I would definitely like to wipe away is having (unprotected) sex on a preacher's desk in his office back in Mississippi when I was younger. So you see I really do feel Paul when he states that he is chiefest of sinners in 1 Timothy: *And the grace of our Lord was exceeding abundant with faith and love which is in Christ Jesus. This is a faithful saying, and worthy of all acceptation, that Christ Jesus came into the world to save sinners; of whom I am chief. Howbeit for this cause I obtained mercy, that in me first Jesus Christ might shew forth all longsuffering, for a pattern to them which should hereafter believe on him to life everlasting. Now unto the King eternal, immortal, invisible, the only wise God, be honour and glory for ever and ever. Amen.*

With that said and read, I know that I can't lose my faith or confidence that God is going to save me from my own chosen lifestyle of sin. I say chosen because I know better but for some strange reason I have chosen to continue in sin. What's my problem? I'm trying to get away from premeditated sin cause I used to be bad at that, but I have to remove myself from the lifestyle completely.

13

SHEILA'S PRAYER FOR US

10:05 p.m. 8/18/04 The Morgan View Lab
Today I really didn't get much work done cause I was making inspirational sheets with various scriptures on it to hang on my wall during the morning and during the afternoon. Ms. Wilming asked me to take a package to Montebello. When I got over there I ran into some people who I knew by face who knew me by name, so that was cool. I had on my salmon colored Polo and my fresh dookies. I was feeling real fly. After I handled Ms. Wilming's business I went about trying to get a bogus meal plan charge removed from my bill. Several of the administrators know me by name now. I also was flirting with this really cute lady and she was feeling me so much that she put everybody on hold. I guess that ain't too cool, but for some strange reason it make me feel good to know that if I had time alone with a lady I could have a good conversation that could lead to who knows what. Pray for me, homey.

Mrs. Nia's twin emailed me and asked if I could send her some more of my journal entries, so I am going to look back and email her an entry that doesn't include her sister. I think she likes me and that's kind of awkward cause I'll never know. She ain't the type to come out and be real with herself and just say it. After work Violet took me back to Midas to pick up my car and one of the mechanics gave me a $15 discount. You know I appreciated that. I drove back to the crib and stopped by the Chinese store up the block before I got home for a shrimp basket. They are usually off the hook, but for the first time my shrimp were burnt. On my way from the Chinese store, it began to rain and that was when I realized that all of a sudden my windshield wipers weren't working. I called the shop and the manager said to bring it in and they would see what they could do. I went home and watched *Mystic River* while eating.

It was raining so hard I didn't think I was going to make it to Wednesday Bible study. Brother Dashings did call me this time, but he didn't call me yesterday, and that sucked cause I was actually waiting on him to call. I was eating and not expecting him to call when he called. Go figure. Anyway, *Mystic River* was good and it was hard trying to figure out who the killer was. I was way off, which is why I like it. Violet came and watched the movie with me and she was her usual self, whatever that is . . . lol. If she ever reads this she would go crazy trying to figure out what that means.

11:25 a.m. 8/19/04 The School of Graduate Studies

Today started off alright and last night was cool too. I didn't smoke or have an urge to smoke, and I went to bed at a decent time. One of my prior friends with benefits came by late to get her DVDs and I knew she wanted to sit and talk for a while, but I put her out and told her I was going to bed. She got mad at me and slammed the door on her way out. When I opened it like I was gone chase her, she broke out. I know she like all that rough and tough stuff and I can give it to her sometimes, but I don't always feel like playing. I really didn't do anything horrible to make myself feel bad, so I fell asleep pretty fast and slept good. I got up this morning and decided to change my whole outfit to a white t-shirt, some Guess shorts and a pair of Adidas. Work is work and when I first got here, I printed out the labels I needed to finish the files that I pulled out to be done, so I should have plenty to keep me from the porn today.

Missy finally got her hats and her money and she sounded happy, so I'm glad for her. Charlene and CJ must have found tickets cause Mom said they are coming out here now, so that is good news. I hung my inspirational scriptures up in my room, so I now feel like I have a sanctuary and am protected from myself with those around. I never know when I may glance at something that may convict me. I haven't been listening to my sermons on tape so I have to get back to that. I chose not to go to church last night, but I will tonight after I take my truck to get the wipers fixed, Lord's will.

The inspirational thought for the day is enjoy the journey. I think I may have enjoyed the journey a bit too much, maybe not. The exercise says to make a list of the great and exciting things happening in my life right now and asks what I am willing to do today to start enjoying these things. Now that is a wonderful exercise because off top I am dumbfounded. God is changing me and He is working on me. Being sober is wonderful, being able to think and deal with folks on a consistent basis cause I ain't high or paranoid is wonderful. The fact that I am able to think is probably the most wonderful gift that God has given me. I feel like I can see through the fog and that is great and wonderful. Even though Satan keeps trying to obstruct my vision, I continue to press on. What am I willing to do to start enjoying these things today? I am willing to go out into the world and let my light shine by spreading cheer and joy to all those willing to accept it.

The scripture for the day is: *God is not a man, that he should lie; neither the son of man, that he should repent: hath he said, and shall he not do it? or hath he spoken, and shall he not make it good?* (Numbers 23:19) This verse reminds me of the verse that says that God is not slack concerning His promises, and if I know this then to apply this in my life I should count it all joy when it looks like there isn't a way because I am supposed to be as confident as Meshach, Shadrach and Abednego in my Lord, knowing that He can make a way out of no way. These are things I need to keep in mind as I stroll through this sinful world.

If I truly believed that then the fear that I have when it comes to speaking to people about God would not arise cause I know He has control of the situation, so this is something I need to work on. The fact that I ain't ran out and told the world how good He is, is a testimony to my beliefs. So pray for me. On a lighter note, heck a much lighter note, I have to get down to business and start focusing on this LSAT, finishing my personal statement and my law school applications cause time is ticking and I don't wanna look up and be behind on any deadlines. Well Ms. Wilming is back here talking to me, so we will hopefully chop it up later, ya undadig?

11:07 p.m. 8/19/04 The Morgan View Lab
Tonight has been awesome for the simple fact that I was entertained alone and I stayed out of harm's way meaning temptation and trouble. Ms. Wilming gave me a microwaveable dinner and a big bowl of spaghetti. You best believe I killed that. I forgot about my truck today and stayed late until about 6:30 cause I ain't going in tomorrow until late because I am going to the dentist and the doctor's office. When I did leave work, I remembered that I had to go back to Midas to figure out what was wrong with my wipers. I smashed down there and was embarrassed cause the dude didn't do nothing but touch my wipers and they started working. I bothered them for nothing and was about to get gangsta with them folks cause I thought they hadn't did a thorough job and had forgot to hook something back up.

After getting my wipers fixed I went back to the crib and prepared my spaghetti and some buttered bread. I also watched the *Last Samurai* and that movie is so good! Oh my goodness! It kinda makes me mad how white folks glamorized and distorted their role in history. They control the media and the movie houses like Paramount so they basically put out any movie they want no matter how twisted they get the story. The movie was good, but you have to remind yourself that it is just a movie because it implies that it really does happen because it almost takes a historically accurate point of view as it incorporates different parts of different history. Tom Cruise acted his tail out and I was actually cheering for him.

I called Charlene and told her the movie was good and she got pissed and was like send me my movie, nigga. I thought that was funny cause it's all love with me and like I told her if she ever comes to Baltimore or to my crib for that matter, she has freedom to take anything she wants cause she my sister and I know she gone take care of it and return it. She wouldn't have to steal or sneak cause I ain't particular about things like she is. On a side note, Mrs. Nia called me talking bout she mad but I ain't trying to hear that. She should be mad cause I wasn't there for her and that makes me feel like less of a man. I almost wish she would leave me alone cause it doesn't feel the same. I mean I wasn't there for her and that hurts and also means I still haven't grown in that part of my life cause I wasn't there for Lala either.

Missy called, and her and B are in Nebraska chilling. I also spoke with Mom tonight and everything is cool with her. I finally got my law school personal statement chopped down to one page. I hope that works. Well I am tired and gotta get up in the morning. Sheila just called and asked if I got her emails. Let me go check.

Boy, that girl is beautiful! This is what Sheila sent me:

> *This is just something that I wanted to share with you.*
>
> *Lord God,*
> *Thank You for sending me Charlie. Forgive us for not keeping our eyes fixed on you. Forgive us for lustful distraction. Please help us to see clearly where you want us to be in our relationship with each other and strengthen our faith that there will be no fear for us to seek you first and to hear your directions clearly. Give us the patience, self-control, strength and joy in You to wait on You.*
>
> *Thank You for Your Son, Thank You God*

What more can I say? She is just beautiful inside and out. I'm not sure if she can handle me, but one day I would love to give her a chance.

14

TALK WITH GOD

2:07 p.m. 8/24/04 The School of Graduate Studies

Breathe is the inspirational thought of the day. How appropriate. The exercise says to practice breathing. It asks if I felt anything different and if so what. Well I just felt that much closer to God my creator and I felt peace come over me. The scripture of the day is: *Prove all things; hold fast that which is good. Abstain from all appearance of evil* (1 Thessalonians 5:21-22). I can apply this by not forsaking his assembly, reading the word every day and resisting the temptation to look at porn on the internet. Let's bow...

Heavenly Father, I come to you at this time giving you all thanks for being such a wonderful and merciful God. Heavenly Father, I thank you for loving me more than I love myself. I thank you for your grace and mercy which you have granted me time and time again even though I am not worthy. Heavenly Father, I thank you for the ability to walk, talk, eat, sleep in peace without shaking, the ability to pray and ask forgiveness and the ability to hear your word and think freely for myself,

Heavenly Father. I thank you for your spirit and the wisdom which you have blessed me with. Lord, I thank you for all of the physical, mental and spiritual blessings which you have bestowed upon me. Most of all I thank you for your mercy cause I know without it you would have had plenty just cause to stop the breath and the blood from flowing through my body. Heavenly Father, I thank you for your Son who has made it possible to even come to you, Lord. I thank you for all the blessings you have bestowed upon me—even those that I don't even know or realize are blessings. Heavenly Father, I come to you humble asking for your forgiveness of my many shameful, stupid and silly sins. Lord, I pray you have mercy upon my soul because I am chiefest of the sinners. I have brought shame upon you and the church and I pray that you will forgive me and have mercy upon my soul. Lord, please hear a sinner's prayer. I thank you for the transportation which you have provided me with and I also wanna thank you for waking me up this morning. Lord, I pray that you keep me humble and ever watchful so that I may not become too complacent in this world and not strive to be the best I can be. Heavenly Father, please help me to forgive those who trespass, lie, cheat, steal and try to hurt me. Help me to walk in your spirit always and to remember that you are always watching me. Heavenly Father, please give me strength to go out and do your will. Grant me the courage and replace my words with your words when the opportunities arise where I can educate someone on you and your word. Lord, touch my mind and my memory so that I may write your word and your commandments in my heart. Help me to not only be a hearer of your word but a doer. Lord, please help me give up the things of this world, the lust and desire of the pleasures of this world so that I may better serve you before it is everlasting too late. Please equip me with the weapons I need to fight against Satan and the lust of the flesh. Help me to recognize Satan and turn away from the appearance of evil, Lord. I ask that you be with Vick. Please bring him out of his current state and bring him peace and joy again, Lord. I ask that if it be in your will to use me that I be ready and willing and that I don't fight against the Spirit. Bless and be with Mom, Tiny, Charlene, CJ and the rest of the family whom I love. Heavenly Father, be with Ma Hill and help her to remember that when man forsake her, you will always be there for her. Lord, be with me as I continue upon this journey. I ask that you bless me if it be your will and this journal so that nothing but good can come out of it. These things I ask and give grateful thanks, in your most precious Son Jesus's name. Amen.

11:19 a.m. 8/24/04 The Morgan View Lab
I went to church and I feel great! I was and still feel delighted that the Lord allowed me another opportunity to hear His word and fellowship with His people. Tonight has been wonderful and I really feel on fire. After work I spoke with Issa on the phone and we had one of the rare good conversations that we have had that lasted a little while. She really thought I was just a great guy and had me on a pedestal as a young boy. I be trying to tell her I was like a preacher's kid, but she can't bring herself to believe it.

Afterwards, I dropped in on a friend from Jersey who was watching *Good Times*. That was interesting, well not really, and I had to dip awfully fast. After leaving there I continued the conversation I had with Issa, then I called Bro. Dashings cause he told me he would call me for church. I ended up calling him three times before he called me back 15 minutes before church started. Satan was working on him cause he had had a long day at work. So I actually helped him win the battle against Satan. We went to church and had an excellent lesson.

After church Missy called and asked if she should send money in to this TV minister and I almost had a fit—not on her of course but in my heart cause she really can be naïve. I got my Bible and began to tell her about Satan having ministers and churches. I eventually told her that the name of the church will ultimately let her know whose church it is. She was very receptive. I just couldn't believe she was going to send money in to have a healing of some sorts. I gave her some scriptures to write down so she could study and I also had her read some scriptures aloud and tell me what she got from it.

15

A MONTH OF SOBRIETY

8:58 a.m. 8/26/04 The School of Graduate Studies

First off, I just wanna say that God is good! This marks the first month I have been sober, straight-up cold turkey, no Black and Milds, no pipes, no blunts, no joints... no nothing! I am so excited and I feel like today is going to be wonderful because deep inside my heart I will keep this fact with me throughout the day. The joyous part about it is I ain't got to tell nobody and I ain't lying or fronting or being deceptive like I used to do in the past when I would declare I had been smoke free for a certain period of time when I was straight up lying cause I was still smoking Blacks or something like that. So this is a real and authentic God-given joy that I feel in my soul, not just a situational and circumstantial joy. I most likely will keep it to myself, cause since I have kept it to myself I haven't had to deal with the hating comments and the serious temptation to help me fall. I have also separated myself from most of the temptation, but continue to pray for me cause I am human. God is good like I said though.

Chanel just came in and politely asked me to do something with the right spirit. This morning in the shower I prayed that God would help me to forgive her for hating as He forgives me, and I do believe He's softened my heart. I know I got to stop allowing her to make me go there cause that's not healthy for my spirit. I called Mom at home this morning because I need a small loan so I can continue on through this month and the next with my participation in the church and its activities and so I can sign up to take this LSAT in October.

Good news! God is good and Satan is a lie! My truck just got towed and I received like three different phone calls letting me know. I don't have enough money to pay them to release it on the spot, so I am just going to let go and let God, but I would like to have my transportation for the youth event at church on Saturday. No worry, I got God on my side and I'm sure I am being sifted because I am trying to walk in the Spirit today. Well I am going to continue pressing on and doing my work to please God and God only. No worries cause greater is He that lives in me than he that lives in the world, so I have faith that God will help me overcome this if it be His will. Pray for me because I am about to go over here and talk to the man responsible for my truck getting towed and ask him why I am always getting singled out. I am not going to go niggafied like everybody expects me to be and I am not going to try and intimidate him. I'm actually going to try and go to him with a gentle spirit. Let's hope between now and the walk over there I can keep Satan out of my thoughts and off my back.

10:35 a.m. 8/26/04 The School of Graduate Studies

I'm back and I still feel joy because I handled the matter the Christian way and I know I will sleep easy tonight if the Lord allows me to live that long. I spoke with Mr. Buttpirate and he really is a hater. He sensed that I was upset or at least that's what he was giving off, but he knew anyway because he helped to create the situation that would try and break my spirit. I saw the devil in his eyes when he said "talk to me" with a grin almost as if he was trying to entice me into jumping on him. I took a deep breath and said I brought Christ with me so I just want a little bit of justice. I explained the situation of how I know he called, and I asked him to be real with me and let me know if I had done something to wrong him or Morgan View because I felt like I was being singled out.

He claimed I wasn't being singled out and that he was just doing his job, how the tow truck has a certain route that it takes to tow the cars and how I just happen to be one of the first. I calmly explained to him that all that was hogwash and he knows it, and I politely told him about all the cars en route to my car that are also in violation. He claims he doesn't know about these so I encouraged him to do his job thoroughly like it seems he does when it comes to my vehicle. He responded, "If you know that there are cars that don't have a permit, tell me where these cars are and I will call and have them towed today." He was just jacking, because he knows I'm a real nigga and it's not in my character to hate on somebody else or snitch. All I could do is tell him to do his job and go out there and look. We had this conversation the last time and he still is acting like he don't know what vehicles I'm talking about.

He knows and I know he knows cause one of the vehicles belongs to a chick who he ate out (slang for oral sex) for free and received nothing in return and she plays him like a lame. I'm quite sure he doesn't know that I know this. I went and told that chick after speaking with him to move her car cause she was hanging around outside the office when I came out probably to see if I snitched, and

I told her I was going to bring him out of the office and help him do his job. I explained to her too that I was protecting her butt and wasn't going to make my case or plead my innocence by incriminating a homey or an associate. She moves so I wasn't snitching or hating, just helping to expose the phony for what he is: a phony and a coward who's not even man enough to admit his hating, a serpent in power.

Anyway I go and ask for two minutes of his time so he can talk to me outside. As soon as we walk out the door, there's a car backed into the first slot with the same sticker as mine and he just looks dumbfounded and says, "Oh, that's supposed to be gone." I'm thinking to myself *You darn right it's supposed to be gone! And a whole lot more are supposed to be gone before me!* But right is right and wrong is wrong like Mom said, so I just have to leave it alone. I called her on my way there to get some wisdom and help keep my spirit and that's basically what she said to me. I'm going to let that brush off my shoulder for now cause if I dwell on it, it will only make me madder and cloud my vision of how good God has been to me today. I have faith that He will get me where I need to be, so I ain't tripping! God giveth and God taketh away!

The theme of the day is: Remember your past, so as not to repeat it. The question asks what situation in your past are you ready to release so that you can move on in your life? As of right now, at this stage in my life, I am ready to release the situation with my mom taking my truck without my permission and getting hit in it. I am able to release it because I now realize she was doing God's work. He used her to take that away from me on purpose to humble me and bring me closer to Him. Had I had it still who knows where my relationship with Him would be. I probably would be deep off in the world or dead. Who knows? But I now know that there was higher purpose for that day, and if the Lord so desires He can give me a vehicle that is 10 times better.

I've been praying for a "better" vehicle but the Lord knows my heart and He will decide when I am ready because a lot of the times we ask for things, but we wouldn't be able to handle them if God gave them to us. We talked about this in Tuesday's men's class. In Psalms 37:4 it reads: *Delight thyself also in the LORD: and he shall give thee the desires of thine heart.* Thing is, when you are delighting in the Lord, your desires and wants will be different from what you think they will be now. The key factor is those new desires will be inline or in tune with God's will. The Lord knows I wouldn't be able to handle a Denali right now because it would be all about me and how many women I can get. He knows my heart, so I thank Him for these times that I am in right now.[14]

God is good all of the time. He is better for me and to me then I am to myself! Another reason that I can release it is because I know that it will help me draw near to God by learning how to communicate better with Him. I have been praying and praying for a new vehicle but there is a scripture for that too. God has known my inner heart for quite some time and this scripture in James 4:1-3 pricked me: *From whence come wars and fightings among you? come they not hence, even of your lusts that war in your members? Ye lust, and have not: ye kill, and desire to have, and cannot obtain: ye fight and war, yet ye have not, because ye ask not. Ye ask, and receive not, because ye ask amiss, that ye may*

---

14 Looking back at this entry is inspiring! God indeed did come through for me in the vehicle department big time. My first vehicle I purchased out of law school was a Cadillac Escalade. I went searching for a Denali, but the one I saw online was sold by the time I made it to the lot. The dealer tried to entice my wife with an Escalade that was recently traded in, but I wasn't going for it. Long story short I ended up getting a steal on the blue Escalade sitting on 22s the dealer was trying to sell my wife. It must've been a dope boy's car because I later learned that it had Aston Martin brakes on it. I also now have a Ford Expedition, and both are fully paid for! Look at God! In the deuces where I grew up in Milwaukee, the only way you were driving an Escalade or an Expedition was by selling dope, scamming or pimping. God has brought me a mighty long way! I know those are everyday vehicles to some, but I got a deeper appreciation for some things given my history, and my vehicles are one of them. At least they ain't minivans! LOL! To God be the glory!

consume it upon your lusts. I have been coveting a Denali for a long time and all the while I have wanted one for my own glory, to feel as if I've made it, keyword being "I've." Not that God has helped me to make it but so I can feel as if I've done something. I have been asking amiss to consume it upon my own lusts, therefore I don't deserve it cause I ain't earned it and I wouldn't be able to handle it if I had it. It probably would bring me more trouble and sorrow than joy so I'm cool. What I have to remember is what is found in Matthew 6:31-33: *Therefore take no thought, saying, What shall we eat? or, What shall we drink? or, Wherewithal shall we be clothed? (For after all these things do the Gentiles seek:) for your heavenly Father knoweth that ye have need of all these things. But seek ye first the kingdom of God, and his righteousness; and all these things shall be added unto you.*

He got my back, my front, both my sides, my top and my low. He's always had me and that's what I have to remember cause I never really needed anything, cause He always took and is still taking care of my needs and quite a few wants! I've been blessed beyond measure and I have to recognize that and keep my focus on Him and He will give me my deepest heart's desire when He has my heart where it needs to be: set on Him.

The scripture for the day is: *Jesus answered and said unto them, Ye do err, not knowing the scriptures, nor the power of God* (Matthew 22:29). How true is that?! I am going to try and change my errors or better yet, submit and let God change my errors cause it ain't no fun struggling when you got a God as good and mighty as the God I serve! I've been bringing misery among myself because I haven't been focused on Him. God is so good.

He can give you joy through a storm if you're focused on Him and got your mind and heart right with Him cause you gone be too busy rejoicing in the fact that He's watering the earth to notice that your perm or yo clothes getting wet. God can give you joy in the presence of your enemies if your mind and heart are right cause you will be too busy rejoicing in the fact that you get yet another chance to show your enemies Jesus and teach about God's word through your actions to notice that you are being hated on.

I ain't all the way there yet, but I'm getting there and I got joy just knowing that one day, Lord's will, I will be there and everything will be alright! Hallelujah! Satan, you can't steal my joy! You can take whatever else you want from me and I'm still gone praise him cause I serve a mighty God and He is able! Matter of fact you might as well hate on me some more cause I'm gone spread my joy and tell others about how good God has been to me! God is good! Oh, I'm snapping, but back to the scripture of the day. When you don't know the scriptures and you ain't studied up, then you don't have no ammo to fight when you fall into situations like mine today.

Good thing I surrounded myself with the word by putting up scriptures in the room cause the scripture that I read today before leaving the room was the one that says: *Greater is He that lives in you than he that lives in the world (1 John 1:5).* Oh how true it is! Since I knew my scriptures, they helped me to remember and realize the power of God through my storm or trial or whatever you wanna call it, and I didn't err by cussing the man out or even losing my Christianity. I handled the situation with grace and poise, and I am even going to pray for him. God is good.

7:58 p.m. 8/26/04 The Morgan View Lab

Boy, Satan is a lie! He's been at me all day about this towing situation and every time I let it die down, somebody else brings it back up. After I left work, I went and talked to Toyketa, the H.N.I.C., and the Lord blessed me through her to receive a new decal for free. God is good. I had to go through some BS and Buttpirate was trying to provoke me, but I was on my best and just brushed my shoulders off. I got the number for the towing company from the front desk and I called to see how much it would cost to get my truck and they said $150. So I called Violet and asked her to take me. She said she was at Jenny's crib and I would first have to go with her to run some errands. Of course, I knew this was going to happen because I needed her and she has to be in control, but I said okay anyway to being held hostage.

I went downstairs to meet her, but she wasn't there yet, but Monique said she would take me and we left. When Violet called, I told her I was cool. I had to stop at the ATM and thank the Lord that the money Mom had put in there had registered (and it allowed me to pull the money out). God is good! So now I can still go to church Saturday! After I got my truck, Monique told me I should write a letter to try and get my money back. So then I did. Lord's will, I will be reimbursed. Well, I am going to walk to the Chinese store and get me a shrimp basket then play Live and watch *The Five Heartbeats*.

16
MR.GOODGAME STRIKES— LOBAN'S TONGUE RING SHORTY

8:21 p.m. 8/28/04 The Morgan View Lab
Last night after getting off work, I drove up to Herb's after playing a game of Live with the intent of scooping Loban for some competition. I ended up staying over there til about 3 in the morning. We sat on the porch for the most part and talked about the hood and different things that go on in the hood. Loban got Herb talking about some events that transpired between Loban's crew and Herb and the football team back in the day and basically we just chilled. Kassy and I can have intelligent conversations and everything be cool, but somewhere in there Loban and Herb went to arguing and debating and the fun just wasn't there anymore. I ended their conversation by approaching our current situation with a how we gone get it crunk attitude.

There was a couple of girls over there and they started playing music, so I went in and started kicking it with them and getting my bug on. One of the shorties was feeling me and started dancing up on me and before the night was over she had me on the ground trying to work it. She and I basically kicked the party off cause we wasn't worried about who was watching or what nobody else was doing. Eventually everyone was paired up, grinding and getting they groove on in the dark. Lil momma who was dancing up on me had to be less than 4ft tall and I wasn't really trying to get down there to dance so she kept coming at me on the couch or floor when I would try to chill. She started hitting the right buttons and I don't know how to put it, but Mr.GoodGame came out. I let her know that there is a reason why I don't dance and that's cause I don't like to be teased. From that point on, it was on. I was in that "other" mode. I convinced her to slip to the crib with me. She was down to go in another part of the house but didn't wanna leave her friend, so I devised the plan that we would slip out of the party to go get some CDs from my crib.

I slipped out but her drunk tail couldn't find her shoes and caught everyone's attention. When I came back in to snatch her up out of the party, she might as well have made an announcement cause we wasn't slipping out no more. We skirted off to the crib and the jumpoff basically jumped off with her tongue ring doing a lot of the initiating. It was decent head and shoulders if I can kind of speak gully for a minute. As we were finishing, I hear the door close. Loban done walked home and the chick all of a sudden gets spooked and starts telling me how Loban like her and be trying to get it, but she just punch him and play him to the left. Loban's cool with her and that's her man; she just don't like him like that and she knew he was going to be salty. She was absolutely right. Although he didn't say nothing, he left his room door open. I guess so he could see and know for sure even though he always come in and close his door. When I walked out, I asked him if he still wanted to get it on in Live and he gave me a dry "Naw, I'm cool" as if he didn't have the heart, will or strength to play.

I drove shawty back to the spot and everyone was on the porch as if they were waiting on us to come back. I was thinking to myself that them niggaz need to get a life. It definitely ain't Milwaukee cause the way things was going, everybody would have separated or slipped off and got a jumpoff—not be outside waiting on somebody else to get back. Another reason why I think Baltimore and its residents are lame. As we came up the steps, they grilled us with that *what was y'all doing* look. We played it off smooth and presented the CDs but it really was for naught cause them niggaz was all on the porch and the party look like it had ended. When we left, it was like the party or the life of the party was gone.

I brought my infamous Kells CD that's guaranteed to get it hot and we brought a little life back to the party. I also brought the Isley Brothers remix CD. Shawty was all up on me after she came back from giving her girl a report on what went down. I'm quite sure that's what went down cause I asked Kassy where she went and she said that they probably was going to talk about my performance. I just laughed cause I always rep me to the fullest. After shawty came back and was dancing on my lap for a while, I hit it on her in the middle of chilling cause it was getting late.

This afternoon I got up, hurried up and got dressed and drove to the Sprint store and put 35 dollars on my bill so my phone would come back on. After paying my bill, I hit it to the church, sweating all the way cause it was 91 degrees out and I ain't got no air in the Escalade.[15] We had so much fun at the go-kart place. We played laser tag and it was about 17 of us total from the church—3 adults and about 14 kids. Me and the boys, when we first got there, got laser tag tickets. While

---

15 Ironically, I used to joke and call my mom's mini-van the Escalade because the back-passenger door slid opened automatically by hitting a button. It was probably the only cool feature in the truck.

waiting for our turn, I tried out the batting cage and I didn't do great. The young boys were laughing and teasing me and I told them that wasn't my sport but basketball was and I would deal with all of them in good time. We went in the arena and played and I killed them fools, so they were amped up and ready to play again, but I told them to wait a lil while. We rode the go-karts next and I came in second. After that, we played laser tag and I won again. This time everybody played except one chaperone. All in all, it was fun!

When I got home, I was so tired that I called Nancy back and told her I wasn't going to make the fair tonight cause I wasn't trying to walk around or sweat again. So now I am searching for LSAT classes because I was reading my LSAT book at the church when we all were meeting to go on the trip and I found out one of the brothers in the church has six years in constitutional law and one of the sisters said she would pay for me to go to an LSAT class. God is good! So that's where I'm at. I am going to find this information then probably play a game of Live, watch a movie and call it a night. Or I might drop by Herb's cause I told Kas I would buy her a drink for her birthday, but I ain't staying tonight.

17

MR.GOODGAME STRIKES AGAIN— ZOE AND THE CLUB

3:34 p.m. 9/2/04 The School of Education Lab
Last night after I left the lab, Zoe, the young lady I met a couple of nights ago when riding with PK and Loban, called me and asked me if I would take them to the club. I laughed and asked them who they thought I was, but they were very persistent on the fact that they wanted to go out and have fun. So I called PK to see what he was doing. Why? I'm not really sure. I let Satan come in somehow. I wasn't watchful and Mr.GoodGame slipped on out before I even knew it. All it took was a measly phone call and the fact that they chose me. Anyhow, PK said he was trying to go to the same club. I hit him with the proposition of he and I doing like a double date so he could experience some good game firsthand cause I think he cool.

The crazy thing is that I think he's cool cause I know he's not a fool. He can wild out at times, but for the most part he's a laid-back type of guy who don't get loud or have to front. The even crazier thing is or the point is he's cool cause I see a little bit of me in him cause although he hangs with the fellas, he goes to church on Sundays. He might be a SMO or Sunday Morning Only Christian or whatever, but the point is he believes in someone other than himself and that's a start. Anyway, he wasn't trying to do that so I told him I would call him back. It's strange how when Satan is trying to get you, how things just seem to pull together to pull you from the Lord. I didn't and wasn't going to drive my van so I decided to try my luck and see if Sherman Merman would let me drive the Honda. Lo and behold, she gave me the keys with no problem or time limit. How ironic is that? I ain't seen her in a couple of weeks, let alone spoke to her on the phone. Mr.GoodGame was in full effect.

I called PK and told him I had wheels and was going to check out the situation. Just like I knew he would, the nigga talking bout he wanted to ride. Me being generous, I told him I would hit him back up. My mind was made up that I was going to go out and have some fun one last time before school officially starts. If I had been in my right mind, I would have known that there is never one last time. You certainly don't prepare for that one last time; it just happens. I ironed some jeans, threw on the fresh Ones, Phillies fitted hat and a white doo-rag, and put on my ghetto fabulous RIP Deuce shirt—Mill Town's finest gear. After getting dressed, I threw some music in a case and headed out to the car. I let the sunroof back, loaded my CDs and hit it. I called Zoe and Lexus then drove to Herb's to see if Loban was there.

To catch you up, Zoe and Lexus are the two cute lil rich Caribbean freshmen from Albany, New York that I met when I hopped out the car about a week ago when riding with PK. Obviously the game was good cause they ended up coming home with me that night. I know it was better than I thought now, cause they called me last night and that's probably what surprised me. Pride will lead to a downfall every time and I was beaming with pride and wanted to brag and tell or show somebody that the game was that good. That's what led me into a storm of trouble last night.

I stopped at Herb's and called the chicks from outside and they said they were already on the bus headed down there, so I went in and Joy said that Loban hadn't been over there all day. I called PK cause I really wasn't trying to go down there by myself and he said to come through. I go through there and Loban and Randy were there playing Live and talking crap. So we figure out how we gone do it and chill til about 12. I drove to the liquor store to grab a Smirnoff cause they were smoking and I wasn't. PK brought the blunt and rode with me cause he thought I was trying to smoke on the low. When I told him I wasn't smoking but he could smoke, he was really like wow. He respected me so much that he put it out and asked if I wanted to hit the Black. I told him again that I didn't smoke, and he really respected that cause he thought I was faking. I explained that I wasn't smoking anything thanks to the grace of God.

It opened up a conversation about God and how good He is and about how eventually just like me he planned to quit, cause he does have some spirituality. He gone realize that there is nothing in this world for him and that he's actually cutting blessings off by smoking. We talked about it and had a real conversation and he was definitely feeling it and actually stopped smoking so we could talk even though I never asked him to and didn't try and make him feel bad. Anyway, after we got back from the liquor store, he hit it a couple times and gave it to Loban which is a start and, for a smoker like PK, is a big deal.

Zoe called and said the line was long and they wasn't letting nobody else in so they would be waiting for me to come get them outside. I laughed that off and eventually we headed down there with Loban and Randy riding in his Acura on 17s, me and PK in the '04 Honda. When we got down there we found two convenient parking spaces right across from the club exit. Oh, and I found my girl and scooped her off the street and boy was she glad to see me! Her friend had left her and went with some dude or that was the story that she gave me at the time. She was shook cause dudes was soliciting her for sex cause she had a halter top and a very mini skirt with some heels. I told her I could see why. We parked and got out, but I told her to stay in the car when she asked if I was going to take her across the street to meet my friends. I told her my friends were wolves and if I introduced her they'd be wondering if I was sharing. I got a kick out of that cause she got my point and was like "It's cool, I'll chill."

She listened to my *Pimping Ain't Easy* CD while I was across the street scrutinizing mud ducks, Carolines and Claire Huxtable types and chopping it up with my niggaz. I would go back to the car periodically to check on her and take a few swigs of my drink. Mind you, I was in Mr.GoodGame mode for real. To put it plainly, I had quenched the Spirit. I goes back one time and she says she wants to go to another club, so I take her down Baltimore Street[16] to one of the strip clubs to see if she ready.

---

16 Baltimore Street also known as "The Block" is a stretch on the 400 block of East Baltimore Street in Baltimore, Maryland containing several strip clubs, sex shops and other adult entertainment merchants. In recent years, The Block has undergone a bit of a revival with the opening of Larry Flynt's Hustler Club and its next-door neighbor Norma Jeans, an upscale urban strip club.

She wasn't and that's good cause although I was in that mode I really didn't wanna turn her out. We went back and she sat in the car and waited on me. On the way back home, I dropped PK off and grabbed Loban and stopped at a gas station to get a pack of Magnums. When we got back, she knew she was spending the night cause I was a beast all night and left no room for doubt. To make a long story short, I blew her back out and got the young head and shoulders, but it wasn't even good or great and definitely not worth the guilt I felt after dropping her off this morning.

Last night I had told her she was a work in progress and she said I made her feel like a prostitute. I soothed that over but scary thing is . . . she likes the way I treated her and she might catch feelings cause she spent the night and was cuddled up under me. I had to tell her to get up off me or get a cover and make a pallet on the floor. This morning after I dropped her off, I was feeling horrible because I had sobered up and was mad at myself cause it was not worth the guilt I felt inside. I fall for the same trick time after time after time, just like I used to do when I was smoking. I tried to stay busy cause I didn't have to be at work until about 3 and it was only about 10:30. I washed dishes, ironed some clothes to wear, studied some tips on the LSAT and took a shower.

In the shower I had a long talk with God and I pray He heard me cause I still had the sin of fornication fresh on my body and in my heart. It was a struggle even trying to talk with him cause the sin was trying to take my thoughts. I stayed in there and prayed for I don't know how long for a repentant heart and for change truly to come before it is too late. After I got out the shower I put some wings and fries in the oven and I started a game of Live. I was Milwaukee and I played against Sacramento and they beat the tar off of me, so I will have to play them again tonight. While I was playing, I listened to one of Brother Gains's tapes and it talked about letting your light shine. It was a good sermon and pricked my heart.

I feel as though I am about to enter a storm because I have been a hearer of the word, matter of fact I've heard plenty, but I haven't been too much of a doer. Although at times I try, I haven't completely submitted or I wouldn't have episodes like last night where I just completely turn my back on the Spirit. That is not good or wise and although my mind says no, I don't have the meekness where I can submit completely and deny my flesh. I say I am entering a storm because after I ate and listened to the tapes, P called and wanted to go on campus and see what's out there and I met him and we went to the campus like I used to do in the old days and looked at all of the skirts and tight jeans and gave our analysis. So pray for me.

The inspirational message of the day is be an inspiration. I might need some inspiration and someone to sharpen me, matter of fact I know I do and I think I am going to have to separate myself completely from myself to evaluate this problem. To be an inspiration is to inspire others with your goodness and love. The exercise asks in what ways can I be an inspiration? I am not exactly sure except checking on my Christian brothers and sisters and letting my light shine to those who aren't in the brotherhood.

The scripture of the day is: *The fear of the LORD is the beginning of knowledge: but fools despise wisdom and instruction* (Proverbs 1:7). How ironic that this is the scripture of the day, because this is the verse I was thinking about in the shower. It's like I'm playing with God and I can't have that much fear of Him if I would play with Him. You don't play with those who you fear. I think Brother Bethem preached a sermon about having a reverent fear of Him a couple of weeks ago. When I am in Mr.GoodGame mode, I think I despise wisdom and I don't be wanting no instructions from nobody unless I don't know where I'm going.

11:13 p.m. 9/2/04 The Morgan View Lab

I just woke up not too long ago. I decided after I got out of class that it would be good for me to just lay it down to stay out of trouble and avoid my phone. That's how Satan got me last night with a call and I wasn't trying to get caught up again like that. When I got home, I got revenge and took my anger out on Sacramento. This time I blew them out cause I was focused. While I was playing, I listened to one of Brother Gains's sermons, but I really wasn't that focused. After the game I got in the bed and slept til 10:30.

Anyway I just got off the bench where I was talking to Mom. This chick who has been writing me on BlackPlanet and who seems to know me but does not look familiar turned out to be the crazy daughter of one of my mom's crazy friends.

Mom them left me a couple of messages warning me about her impersonating someone else to talk to me, so I handled that call first. I got several calls while I was sleep but didn't answer. I told Mom about what happened last night and she was asking for details and had me talking my business outside. I was sharing with her how it happened and why. Of course she was trying to give me advice, but I was getting emotional cause I know that I was wrong and she was telling me I was wrong and what I need to do. My problem is I know what I need to do; I just don't do it sometimes.

As we were talking, Sherman Merman had her window open and hollered out for Loban, but I know she knew it wasn't Loban cause I don't sound nothing like him. She was basically letting me know she knew I was down there and that she heard me. That sucked cause I was talking some real ish to Mom, so that kind of upset me. She was in the window when she said it with a nigga that Loban introduced me to. He lame but the point is I don't want nobody, especially no one that can't help me, to know what I'm going through. After that I was trying to get off the phone cause Mom was in the Spirit, touching me with her words and asking open-ended questions.

After I got off the phone I spoke with Missy briefly and then Zoe called talking bout she bored. She told me she had just got back from dropping a letter to her ex-boyfriend in the mail. It's crazy, but I seem to have that effect on women. I think I am going to have to apologize and tell her I was out of character and out of line and keep it real and let her know how I am trying to grow up and get away from that old lifestyle. Maybe she will see my struggle and make it easy on me by leaving me alone. That leads me to where I am at now: the lab. I still feel like I gots to get me something to eat, so that could lead to trouble but hopefully I can have some self-control and tap my sources without literally tapping my sources.

If I didn't tell you in the beginning, I really was—and I say was cause once I get right I ain't trying to turn back to my vomit—a beast, a roaring lion seeking whom I can devour, a wolf and a true straight up hood nigga who for fun banged pros, smoked weed and got money, no matter how grimy the means of getting it was. Pray for me. Lord, have mercy on my soul and help me not to take your grace for granted.

18

MR.GOODGAME THE SAVAGE

10:45 a.m. 9/3/04 The School of Education Lab

I am so pissed at myself. Why did I do it again? I fell for the same trick and put myself in a position to fail. Why did Lexus, Mona's friend, call me late last night and say that they both wanted to come over and kick it? My twisted mind automatically jumped to ménage à trois and I went and got 'em. They got me some chicken and fries at Stoccos but it wasn't really all that. We went to my crib and I ate my chicken and watched *Ocean's Eleven*. Lexus left midway through the movie, leaving me and Mona all alone. I told her after the movie I wasn't trying to take her home and that she would have to spend the night. Why did I do it again? I resisted having sex with her cause the last time I was with her I told her I need head and shoulders to get me motivated. She wasn't trying to do that last night, so I just went to sleep. When we woke up this morning she had her butt pressed up against me and stirred it enough to gently wake me up. Well I still wasn't trying to do nothing without head and shoulders. Eventually she gave in and I reluctantly had sex with her. My conscience was warring the whole time. I even turned my back on her several times to resist, but I'd set myself up for failure because before I went to sleep I put in my infamous R. Kelly CD. It's ironic cause at the time that it jumped off, "Bump and Grind" came on at the part where R. Kelly sings "My mind's telling me no, but my body is telling me yes."

I am so pissed at myself. It wasn't even good. She got hers and I ain't get mine. I couldn't even pray this morning in the shower cause I knew better but didn't do better! It don't do no good to know better and not to do better. I then also started thinking about something Mom asked me last night: How you gone take an HIV test last week and still continue in your old ways? Good question, I guess it's just foolishness. Pray for me.

I started not to include the scripture of the day in this journal entry cause I forgot my inspirational book and I usually do them together, but I am glad that I didn't cause I need this scripture of the day. It reads: *Brethren, I count not myself to have apprehended: but this one thing I do, forgetting those things which are behind, and reaching forth unto those things which are before, I press toward the mark for the prize of the high calling of God in Christ Jesus* (Philippians 3:13-14).

I got to press forward and do my best to submit to His will and resist Satan. STAND UP! This is what I must tell myself. Stand up and let your light shine before men. It is kind of hard to do when you got guilt on your heart and you're separated from the Spirit. I have to continue pressing forward regardless though. God will forgive me if I can forgive myself. I've fallen into Satan's guilty trap too many times before. I just don't know if I should repent or just do my best to make it through the weekend until Sunday. Either way I have to press forward and do all the good I can do.

12:18 a.m. 9/6/04 The Morgan View Lab
This weekend I've been running so much that I haven't had a chance or I didn't create an opportunity to report back to the journal. I'm not sure where to start and it's late, so I'm sure I will not be able to fit it all in this one sitting. Anyway, let's see . . . Friday, I left work for lunch and came back to the crib to chill out. P came through and we went on to the campus to loiter and ran into PK. Since P had to go to work, I decided to go over PK's and play the game for a while. Don't ask me what I was thinking or what my logical reasoning for this decision was because I was supposed to have reported back to work and talked with Chanel about

Mrs. Katie's grades, but I just ignored all of those responsibilities. I was wilding and I can put it no other way. PK beat me the first two games we played on Live cause he had a better team and we were playing his view. The third game we played half and half, meaning the first half we played in his view and the second half we played in mine, and I won. We switched to football and I ended up slaughtering him, although he was talking mad tough cause I only played it twice.

He left while I was in the middle of a game with Hov. When he got back, he said his taillight had went out and he couldn't take me home cause it was dark, so I was stranded waiting on Randy to get off work at 11 o'clock. When Randy finally came home, that nigga was acting drunk so I had to call P. When P got over there, him and Gabe wanted to play some Madden, so I just got on the floor and told them to wake me when they got ready to leave. I ended up getting home at about 4:30 a.m. That sucked cause my Friday was very unproductive and boring. I didn't get a chance to clean the apartment or wash my clothes, but I really wasn't sweating it like that. That was what I got for wilding.

Saturday was much better though, cause I got up and Nancy came through and we went to the church picnic. We stopped and got some Popeye's before we went out there and it took us like 45 minutes to get there cause it was so far out. I hadn't eaten, cause when you say picnic the first thought I get is food. Why eat my food when I ain't got much? I didn't eat breakfast before I left, so when we did finally get there I was starving. I proceeded to make me a plate out of the food that I had bought, just a snack. But when folks seen me start eating, they attacked the Popeye's box and we had to pray before things got out of order. I started the jump off and I had to apologize cause I had only wanted to put something on my stomach but the true character came out of some of the members and I had opened the flood gates for the food to be devoured.

Anyway, we had fun at the picnic. We played spades, football and volleyball. I was killing in the spades of course and both games I played, I was winning when the opposing partners decided that they had something else to do or made some excuse to leave. I saw Brother Clint's wife and Nancy trying to put together a volleyball net and they really looked pathetic cause both are barely five feet and wasn't nobody trying to help them, so I went and helped them get the net. After we got the net up, we went to playing with the people who wanted to play. One of the brothers who I didn't really know but was talking junk to (out of love) got baptized this evening and I really do feel it's because when I saw him in church this morning he came up to me and I actually remembered his name and where I knew him from. The smile he gave me let me know that he felt the love. He also seen me serving today because they finally decided to let me do something and I was on the Lord's table doing the Lord's supper as an assistant. It's a start and you got to start somewhere.

After the picnic, Nancy and I dropped two of the young teenage boys off at home and had a nice talk on the way home. When we got there I could tell she didn't want to leave but my room was a mess and my sheets were still dirty from Zoe, so I stopped that idea early. I went in and got freshened up and walked to the game and just mobbed by myself for a hot minute. I think I actually was receiving a lot of love cause I was dolo and everybody comes to the game deep cause of various reasons. I ran into Loban and P and chilled with them for a hot minute until the end of the game then I ran into Violet and Mrs. Sunshine. I ain't talked to Mrs. Sunshine in a while and it was refreshing to see her again. Violet left a sour stench in the air cause she be acting bourgie sometimes like she better than other people and that gets tired to me. I start acting cocky intentionally to rub her the wrong way and send her on her way. That's what I eventually had to do because she really can't stand alone and I don't respect that at all.

I ended up sitting out on the bench with Loban looking at chicks while P was taking his pops and lil brother home. When he got back, he was ready to get into something and my eyes hadn't had their fill. Although I saw plenty eye candy, my soul had seen enough and I knew I was serving at church in the morning cause Brother Clay told me Wednesday night. So I left them cats and walked home and got my clothes ironed for church.

They took a detour to the liquor store then came to the room, but I set the mood with my church music. They saw me ironing and P asked what I was doing, and I let him know. Satan was in him on the low, but I had my mind made up and I wasn't ashamed, so he had to find a different approach. I think with my determination, Satan had to leave me alone, but he took one last swing to let me know he was there. When P and Loban were leaving to go smoke and drink on the picnic bench, P said, "Alright my nigga have fun at yo ish tomorrow." I looked at him like *Satan, get gone*. He said, "My bad. You know I didn't mean to call it ish, but you know what I mean." I said, "Yeah, I got you. Y'all be safe tonight. I'll holla." And that was my Saturday night.

Now Sunday was beautiful. I made it to church on time for Sunday School. I served and treated myself to Old Country Buffet for lunch in between services. The young brother got baptized, and me and Brother Dashings were literally the last ones to leave. Matter of fact, Brother Bethem told us to turn out the lights when we leave, jokingly referring to the street lights. I got back home washed some clothes and talked with Missy, Nancy and Brother Dashings about how I feel that Nancy is really taking to me, but I want to keep it Christian because I have no interest in her at all. She is just a beautiful spirit who reminds me of Mom. Anyway, it is really late and I am going to get out of here.

1:28 p.m. 9/6/04 The Morgan View Lab

God is good and very merciful! Today started off wonderfully although last night didn't end with the best. Zoe came over last night and spent the night. Why I let her come over, I have no idea. She walked over though and I wasn't taking her home and I told her this. She's lonely cause her homey Lexus went home for the holiday. Anyway, she was a big burden and I didn't want to share my bed with her. I sinned with her last night and that's why I said the night didn't end good. This morning I had my mind right and I woke up upset at myself but prepared to do what I had to do and that was put Zoe out. I had to do her like Tiny cause she had her butt all on me and her lil bony self wasn't trying to get up, so I snatched the cover off of her and nudged her in her ribs until she got up. After pleading with me for a while to sleep longer and for me to drop her off, she left.

Mom and Charlene both called this morning and woke me up. Charlene wasn't talking bout nothing and let me go back to sleep, but Mom called back like 10 minutes later and didn't want to let me go. We were having a good conversation and she was dropping knowledge, but sometimes you just don't wanna hear it. I listened though cause she was dropping jewels. She had read my journal and come to a conclusion that I've known for a while: I am borderline depressed. I also thought for quite some time that I may be bipolar cause I have extreme highs where Mr.GoodGame takes over and I feel like I own the world or I am myself and I feel totally entrenched by the Spirit and I know that I can do all things through Christ who strengthens me. There are times where I am Mr.GoodGame, running from whatever by drinking, smoking and having sex. Then there is me where I feel the responsibility to teach the world and share the knowledge I have and I really don't wanna do it and I get depressed. Either way though, the stuff Mom said was on point. I was just sleepy and focused on getting Zoe from under me.

After Mom's call, I called Brother Dashings cause we were supposed to be going out to breakfast this morning but he was sleep. He called me back later and we spoke and I told him he gone put me on his wife's bad side by having me calling there for him and him not answering the phone. I didn't call too early. It was about 11:45 but still. Anyway, I am waiting on Nancy to come and get me for this cookout, so I have to keep the words short.

10:08 p.m. 9/6/04 The Morgan View Lab
The cookout was off the chain! There was plenty of food, games and fun and good Christian fun. The food was off the chain though. I played quite a few games of basketball with the young bucks of the church and a couple of them had some game. Anyway, Violet and I are about to go to Applebee's so I am going to have to continue this later...

19

APOLOGY TO NIA AND HIV TEST RESULTS

12:08 a.m. 9/7/04 Violet's Laptop
Wow! What a trip to Applebee's! Violet and I had a real talk about different issues and boy what a conversation it was! The issue was that she feels that I have a better than thou attitude and I found that real funny because I know I'm not the only one who thinks that she is like that. We will come back to that in a minute, but I just thought about a conversation that me and Brother Dashings had last night about Nancy. He told me to be careful and I let him know that ain't nothing popping like that cause she is not my type. Anyway, he warned me about some things not to do and to do to make sure that I don't send her mixed feelings. One thing he warned me about was accepting gifts and I let him know that I wasn't taking any gifts and I was rolling dutch with her on everything.

It was ironic that we had that conversation cause this afternoon when she came to pick me up, she handed me a gift bag! Oh, Lord! Usually I am elated to get gifts from anybody, especially females, but because of Brother Dashings's forewarning I really became worried. I told her I can't accept it and she said it was just a gag gift. I didn't wanna take it and lead her on, but she had the look like if I didn't take it her heart would be broken. I still let her know that I didn't wanna accept the gift and that she couldn't be giving me gifts cause I ain't no gift giving person and my memory sucks. I think she got the point and I made it very clear that I wasn't going to be accepting any gifts from her.

We also went and got Jack, the outcast of the church who comes in long white t-shirts and is from the straight up hood. After the cookout, Jack came to my house and we freestyled and bonded. I let him borrow two DVDs and gave him two packs of cigarettes that I took from Sherman Merman and 20 dollars. He stays in a shelter during the week and that is why he misses church. To prevent that, I told him that he could always come over and chill at my crib. Meanwhile, Violet is still talking to me about how she is losing friends and how people are disregarding her and she is really hurt. I am being a friend by staying here and listening, but I kind of knew it was coming because she is so cautious and worries so much that she pushes people away. I told her one day she would learn that this world is a funny place.

Side note, while I was with Violet I ignored a call from Missy. Sherman Merman also called me and told me she would hit me back in about a half an hour which is why I am staying and listening (to make the time go faster). I need to talk with Sherman Merman cause I tried to give her some game about how to deal with P and she just couldn't handle it. The other day when I walked up on her and P, she was telling him that someone said that he called her a hoe and although P knew it couldn't have been anyone but Loban or me, he was too scared and knew better than to come at me.

My thing is I gave you the knowledge to empower you. Knowledge is power and you don't have to share your knowledge with a person cause that's what gives you power over that person. As soon as you share it, you just lost your power over them. Since she didn't want the power, my thing is don't try to start no drama or I will end it quickly, and that is the reason I was going to talk to her. Violet is still talking . . .

10:58 a.m. 9/7/04 The School of Education Lab

Today started off early for me. Brother Dashings called me at 7:30 because I challenged him to be a leader and set the example on how a prayer partner is supposed to be and I would follow him. Well, he sure set an example and got me back for all the pressure. He called me early this morning to let me know he called cause he thought I thought he wasn't going to call, so I am glad that I provoked him unto good works. I wasn't so glad about it this morning, but I am grateful nonetheless. We had a good conversation even though I was groggy. We talked about walking in the Spirit and the verse that he read and gave me for the day was Romans 12: 9-12, which reads: *Let love be without dissimulation. Abhor that which is evil; cleave to that which is good. Be kindly affectioned one to another with brotherly love; in honour preferring one another; Not slothful in business; fervent in spirit; serving the Lord; Rejoicing in hope; patient in tribulation; continuing instant in prayer.*

The main verse that we are going to focus on today though is verse 12 which is going to help me today because I am going to rejoice in hope concerning some thoughts that I have been having about the test I took a couple weeks back. I am going to be patient in tribulation and continue instantly in prayer when something goes wrong or I feel the Spirit losing ground to the flesh. Satan has been trying to put worrying thoughts in my head concerning the test results, but God doesn't give us a spirit of fear but one of love. Fear is false evidence that appears real, so I am telling Satan to get behind me. I am going to call for my results today and also have to call and schedule an appointment to get my wisdom tooth removed tomorrow or sometime soon cause I am out of penicillin. I am truly blessed to have a prayer partner like Brother Dashings because he is a seasoned Christian.

Although I haven't spoken with her, I have been thinking about Sheila because I believe I am ready to make that move. It's not when I believe I am ready though; it's when God feels I am ready. I spoke with Brother Dashings about preaching, and he will be preaching this Sunday evening and he has been preparing himself this week. He was telling me how he puts his sermons together and it made me realize Satan has been trying to prevent me from putting sermons together for the longest because I have surrounded myself by them and ideas for them because of all the inspirational books that I've read to try and help keep me balanced. Next thing that I have to do is mortify this flesh and I am good to go. That's easier said than done, but I can do all things through Christ who strengthens me.

I really do believe if I had a wife to hold me down, who actually knew me and could handle me, I could preach and walk the walk as well as talk the talk. I think that is why I have been thinking about Sheila. For some strange reason, (maybe due to guilt) I also called Mrs. Nia and apologized to her this weekend for any drama, mess or pain that I have caused her. She broke up with her boyfriend for me and look at how I did her. I couldn't even afford to help her pay for the abortion that she had, and I haven't seen her or really made an effort to see her since she told me she was pregnant. When I reap what I have sown . . . boy, it is going to be hell on me! All I can do is beg God for mercy and forgiveness. Anyway, those are serious thoughts and deep issues that I think I am going to have to deal with because for some reason when I am told by a young lady that she is pregnant, there is never joy; I feel contempt and mistrust toward her all of a sudden. I did it to Lala and Nia, and it makes me wonder what's really going on.

Anyway, that stuff is deep and I want to get on a lighter note. We are having game night at the church and we are going to play PS2 and have snacks for the kids. Of course I am a kid at heart and I look forward to the competition and joy that I get from being around Christians and knowing I have to set an example. Side note, I didn't get any studying in on my LSAT this weekend, but I am going to try to make up for it this week. I also am going to pay my rent, Sprint, and try to sign up for the LSAT class this week which will leave my funds low.

The scripture of the day is: *Seeing ye have purified your souls in obeying the truth through the Spirit unto unfeigned love of the brethren, see that ye love one another with a pure heart fervently* (1 Peter 1:22). This is one verse that I have no problem applying to my life because when I am in the Spirit, I am in the Spirit and I show my love to even those who don't want it. I forgot my inspirational book so I will have to pick up on that next time.

4:09 p.m. 9/7/04 The School of Education Lab
God is good and whoever started the saying that He treats us better than we treat ourselves was not lying! I just got back from my lunch break and prayer truly does work because I redeemed the time. In that short time, I paid my rent by going to get the money order, scheduled an appointment for next Monday to finally have my tooth pulled, and I received the results from an HIV test that I took. I didn't talk about it much in the journal because I have been letting other people read this and that was truly a big fear of mine. Satan was really messing with my head regarding that

and I was really having a struggle fighting off the thoughts of my past. After I took it, I wondered why I did it. It was like asking a question that I didn't want to know the answer to.

God has been good though because He gave me things to do to keep my mind off worrying. God has been better to me than I've been to myself because I actually expected to have HIV because of the number of times I've had sex and the number of partners. I have had a super extensive sexual history and about the only playeristic or pimpish thing I haven't done involving sex is a ménage à trois. Boy, I was having thoughts of getting positive results then knowing who truly loved me cause I would tell everyone that I knew I had unprotected sex with like LaLa, Quin and Missy. If I had it, then they would probably have it and therefore I might as well marry whichever one still wants me and doesn't wanna kill me. When I say I was shook, know that deep down inside somewhere I had some worrying thoughts and had to tell myself constantly when those thoughts surfaced that God doesn't give us a spirit of fear. I was thinking about Rihanna from Shubutta, Becky the white girl from Wabo, whose dad was a top ranking KKK member, and Lisa who I did in the grass of Vick's backyard on 5th when he wouldn't let me in. I thought of so many instances where the girls' sexual history was very questionable from the way they let me treat them and I really had to pray that He would take the spirit of fear and worry from me. God is good and He kept my mind busy and off of those worries.

Well now that that is out of the way and I know I am clean, I can't dirty myself up. I got to remain pure cause that means I can have kids and I have something to bring to the table if married. God is good. So now my focus is to keep myself pure, sort of like smoking cause this has been a huge scare for me and I don't want to have to have something disastrous happen before I wise up. It has been quite a hectic and stressful past couple of weeks as far as these tests are concerned because I didn't want to put it in the journal and accidentally send it off and then have Mom or Charlene talking to me about it and bringing my thoughts back to the forefront when I was trying my hardest to push all those thoughts to the background. Since I wasn't releasing it in the journal, holding this stuff inside really did a number on me, but I thank the Lord that I am able to breathe easy and continue on with life ever knowing that He spared my ignorant tail again when I didn't deserve it.

20

SHERMAN MERMAN AGAIN . . .

4:01 p.m. 9/10/04 The Morgan View Lab
Last night was not a good night and Mom gave me the warning when I spoke with her. She asked me what I was doing up and why I wasn't going to bed. After creating my last journal entry, I wound up at Sherman Merman's crib. She called me and asked for a razor so I took her one, but she wasn't trying to use it then and was trying to keep my stuff. I needed something in return so I took 2 DVDs but she was nagging about them, so I took the new R. Kelly bootlegs that she had and she was cool with that. I was going to take them and she was trying to get them and the next thing I know she unzips my pants. Immediately my conscience kicked in and I spoke up about my test results like I just got a fresh start and I ain't messing it up like that, but she was very persistent and I ended up committing fornication with her. Of course, me being weak and not using my proper head just complied.

I felt like crap and Satan was jumping all over me and my thoughts. When I got back to the room to take my mind off what had just happened, Jack and I played Need For Speed II Hot Pursuit where

I was the cop and he was the criminal. Of course, I caught him each time then we played a game of NBA LIVE 2004 and I won that too. When I woke up this morning, Satan was riding me again and I had to tell him to get behind me. I prayed and asked for forgiveness in the shower. I ironed some jeans and threw on my salmon colored Polo because Dr. Tailor, Monique and I had a meeting with a representative from The Adler display Board Company. That went well on the account that I was there because Dr. Tailor is still a bit rough around the edges. Afterwards she treated us to Bennigan's and I now have the itis and can barely stay woke. That's why I came back to the crib so I could hurry up and get this entry out the way cause I need my rest for tonight.

The inspirational message for the day is Be Present. Hmm . . . the exercise asks how can I be present today? Well, I can redeem the time and make the most of the day after I wake up from my nap. Oh yeah, I got some studying on the LSAT in and got a good understanding about what the logical reasoning portion of the tests will be looking for.

21

MR. GOODGAME QUICKIE AFTER CHURCH WITH ZOE

9:30 p.m. 9/12/04 The Morgan View Lab
God has granted me another day which I know I didn't do anything to deserve. Today was a blessed day because Jack and I were leaving for church right on time and I got a call from Alicia, one of my neighbors downstairs in my building. She wanted a ride to church. She was supposed to have been going with this other cat, but he stood her up and had her waiting in front of the building all dressed up. Brother Bethem preached a wonderful sermon on several different topics. He was in the Spirit so he related his sermon to everything and it was like he was talking to the visitors. He was talking bout female preachers and why we don't have a piano and a choir. It was just a wonderful sermon. We made it just in time to church for me to serve cause they had just given my position away when I walked in. He saw me and was like "There he go." This time I knew exactly what to do and it felt good to put in work for the Lord.

I had to repent before serving on the table though, so when the time came where they give you a chance to repent, I stood up. I really felt convicted because yesterday at the game, Alicia heard me say b-i-t-c-h to Violet and that was all I could think about. I'm glad she came to church with me or I probably would have sat there and worked the Lord's table without repenting aloud. I've felt myself wilding all week and I really did an introspective look at myself today during the sermon. After church, Alicia was ready to jet and was kind of anti-social. She looked uncomfortable without me so it made me kind of question her motives for going. Did she think she was just going to be hanging on my arm looking good or did she just think it was a chance to get some alone time with me like we were on a date? I don't know but I want to talk to her tonight and find out how she liked her experience. I didn't like the way she was rushing me so I stuck her with JuJu while I made my rounds. After church we came home and went our separate ways. Me and Jack went to the room and heated up some leftovers that his mother gave me last night. After eating, we took naps and prepared for the evening worship service. Getting up for evening worship seemed like it was hard for both of us, but we made it and were on time too.

During evening worship, I sat next to the youngster who beat me in Live on Friday and that was all he could talk about. I think I was a good example for him though cause I was singing, taking notes, focusing and making him focus and do what I was doing. Brother Dashings was the preacher, so I was very attentive because I wanted to see how his week of preparation had prepared him. He gave about 30-something scriptures and it was a Bible marathon. After church Nancy explained to me how she had been praying for me, how she felt I had a beautiful spirit, and how she prayed that I wouldn't be caught up in trying to help someone else and lose my spirituality. I told her to keep praying for me and not to worry.

Afterwards Jack and I went to McDonald's and I spoke to him about 2 Thessalonians 3. The chapter that talks about separating from a brother who has a disorderly walk and the man who doesn't work doesn't deserve to eat. I gave him the choice to either put down the weed and try his hardest to follow the Lord or get back at me when he can make that commitment. I gave him til tomorrow to make up his mind cause I didn't want to seem harsh, but I did explain to him about my spirituality and how him smoking around me and us kicking it wasn't good for me. The reason was because the beast is more prone to come out with him around because he ain't really striving to be Christ-like and therefore it wasn't a real challenge for me to let the beast out cause he would blend right on in. Satan knows my weaknesses and when we got home, Lexus and Zoe had called about four times. I called Zoe and she said she was walking over to my crib to get her earrings. I sent Jack to the store prior to her calling to get some more incense. I went and let her in the gate, and just in that small amount of space, Mr.GoodGame came out when I saw her. I asked if she was down for a quickie, and of course she said yes. So that is where I am at right now, still spotted with sin and iniquity. Pray for me. I told Jack that he couldn't smoke in the crib anymore. Hopefully I will be able to provoke him unto good works. If not, he gots to bounce. Pray for me. Still smoke free.

*

To overcome my addictions, I needed to change my environment. I changed mine by taking down the *KING* magazine centerfolds and putting up scriptures. Like the BET show starring Gabrielle Union, *Mary Jane*, the scriptures helped me reaffirm who I was and whose I was. I began to love myself again because I remembered that God loves me despite my many flaws. I also learned how to be content being alone and enjoying my own company. If you aren't your own best company, you may need to reevaluate your life.

However, the more I began to love myself, the more pride reared its ugly head. Proverbs teaches that pride comes before a downfall and my pride often came in the form of Mr.GoodGame. When Mr.GoodGame came out I almost always fell into sin because I would aggressively pursue the fulfillment of my flesh to feed my ego and pride.

Interestingly, an idle mind is the devil's playground. It's important that when you change your environment and isolate yourself, you have good people who will help you to walk in your purpose around you. Brother Dashings and the other members of the church helped me not to give up on the Lord or myself when I fell. When you are alone, and you have fallen, guilt, worry and your thoughts can stress you out. Science has shown that stressing can make you physically sick. To overcome my addictions, I had to learn to quiet the negative thoughts in my head. This means you have to watch what you let in your mental environment. As the saying goes, "garbage in—garbage out." The Bible tells us to guard our heart or mind because your thoughts can define your destiny. Today, I make certain that my kids understand the message of a poster on my wall that says:

"Watch your thoughts; they become words. Watch your words; they become actions. Watch your actions; they become habits. Watch your habits; they become your character. Watch your character; it becomes your destiny."

This is why it's critical that in addition to having good folks around you, you must fill your thoughts with positive affirmations. One of the books that my wife and I published through our company to ensure our kids know this lesson is *12 Affirmations for the Amazing Kid.*[17]

---

[17] www.thelittlebrownbiblestorybook.com

22

EXPOSED?

1:32 p.m. 9/20/04 The School of Education Lab
Drama! Drama! Drama! That is the word of the day, but we will get back to that later. Knowing that God can fix anything, that is who I will turn to. The scripture of the day is: *I pray not that thou shouldest take them out of the world, but that thou shouldest keep them from the evil. They are not of the world, even as I am not of the world. Sanctify them through thy truth: thy word is truth* (John 17:15-17). Well it feels like this verse can be applied to my life in my current situation. Although I am trying to do right, I am still in this evil world and it is not going to be easy trying to straighten up because Satan's people are watching and waiting on me to slip. I have to stay in God's word to sanctify myself and around God's people. I get the feeling that I better run for shelter because Satan sees too much good influence coming out of me and he is going to try to stop me from winning souls to Christ by any means possible. So I gots to keep my head up and keep the faith no matter how Satan tries to shame me. I gots to be like Job and stay steadfast.

The inspirational thought for the day is Spontaneity. I have nothing to say about that at this point because there are other more pressing thoughts and matters that I must address so I can get them down and release them. Today started off good. I got up and had a nice talk with my Father in the shower. I already knew what I was going to wear so I was very time efficient in getting out of the house this morning. I checked my messages as I walked to work and had a message from Granny Hill that wasn't one of the most uplifting messages that she's left me. It sounded like she was going through something. She had called Mom and Charlene and neither had answered so she called me. Since I didn't answer she just felt really bad and said that she thought we were her family and that she wanted to talk to us. She called early in the morning when I was sleep, and I'm sure Charlene and Mom were sleep because she said she called in the morning. Anyway, when I got to work, I checked my MSN email and this is the email exchange I had with Nia who I mentioned earlier in the journal:

From: Me
To: Her
Subject: What's going on?
Date: Wed, 15 Sep 2004 10:49:21 -0500

I got your voicemail but the radio and the background noise was so loud that I could barely hear you. I left you 2 messages to call me but since you haven't I am going to try another form of communication. On the voicemail it sounded like you said someone, I think Chanel, said I was saying bad things about you. Fact of the matter is that I haven't said one bad word about you and you always gone be my roadie no matter what. I ain't said much about you at all, but if I did say something about you it was all positive. And no I ain't told our business. The only possible thing that I would have said about you was that I missed you. Other than that, you are getting some hogwash and I want to talk to you so you can tell me what you heard. Please contact me because I have enough trouble in my heart concerning the things that we have been through. That's my word though. I ain't never had nothing bad to say about you and it hurt me when I got your message. It hurts to think after what we've been through and the experiences we've had that you would even think I am capable of flipping like that on you. I take that as you telling me in so many words that I'm phony and I don't take too kindly to that, so you need to get back at me and justify your remarks. Slanging accusations and making threats, I forgot about that part, but it sounded like you said something about I need to watch out cause I could get hurt which I took as a threat. So you definitely need to get at me because unlike some folks I expect better of you and he or she who answers a matter before hearing the whole issue brings shame upon themselves, Proverbs something . . .

From: Her
To: Me
Subject: RE: What's going on?
Date: Mon, 20 Sep 2004 11:53:31 -0400

First of all, I do think that you are phony. I don't know anyone, not even my worst enemy who would have left me in THAT time of need and not even volunteer to pay something. I just don't understand you. I don't. You didn't even try to come down to see me. You always left it up to me like if I don't come see you then we just won't see each other. What kinda bull is that? Whenever you want something, you never have a problem getting it. Obviously you didn't want to see me or you would have.

People who never knew about me and you, cause I didn't say anything to anyone, has come up to me telling me personal things about you and I and have also told me things that you have said. And just as a word of advice: When you have personal feelings or thoughts that you need to write down, don't write them (type them) on a PUBLIC COMPUTER! I know all about you. You are nothing but a player and I'm glad that I never fell in love with you or you would have broken my heart. You take what you want from others but never volunteer to do anything for them. I don't remember you doing anything for me (big or small). Other people also know about you.

So just leave me alone. I went through the hardest part of my life by myself (thanks to you). Now I'm fine and I would rather leave bad memories in the past.

My response back was:

OK, that's that. Whatever, I just think you are looking to start drama, but if not . . . hey, it's all good. I never intended to hurt you and to this day I never spoke a bad word about you, I don't know if someone found our memoirs, my journal or what and that's all fine and dandy because I only speak the truth, but I never said one bad thing about you to anybody and I know how to keep my business to myself. All the rest of that hate directed toward me will take care of itself. As far as the money is concerned, Nia, I didn't have it and that is the straight up honest truth. As far as me being a player, I never professed to not be a player or ladies' man. Matter of fact when we first met I warned you that I was experienced with ladies and that I usually had a way with them. I ain't try to tell you that you were the only one I was talking to. I did think you were different though, but I guess I was wrong too. I ain't never been one to make enemies or try to make enemies so that's why I am responding because I don't want you to think I came after you with malice in my heart or hate. If you think you know so much and believe the people who you are getting this information from, why don't you ask for the information yourself? Sherlock. I know you wouldn't be coming at me like this if you had the facts. You are just going by what someone says and that's all good cause they are telling you stuff that they couldn't possibly know. But I expect you to be smarter and wiser than that. When people are trying to start some mess and Satan is working, he ain't gone mention nothing good or even the truth. He's going to pick and choose what information he wants to disseminate. So I think it is obvious that somehow someway one of the snakes in that office, and you know most of them are snakes. They have tracked down either our memoirs, which I doubt or my journal, which is a little bit more personal. So if that is the case (it's probably old or should I say part of the early beginnings) and you want to know the truth and you think these people are telling you to help you or uplift you or open your eyes ask them to email you what they got. It's as simple as that. Don't come at me from left field threatening me and my integrity. I bet you if you get the information for yourself, and I got it and could send it to you but then you would probably think it is edited, then you will change your tune because I kept my business to myself and I only speak the truth and what I feel. Now that's the end of that . . .

I addressed that matter and feel Satan is trying to sift me, and God has allowed him to for whatever reason because I am quite sure (or at least I was) that I had erased all my information off that computer. Matter of fact, my last day was dedicated to erasing pictures, music and documents off that computer. I guess the Lord sees fit to have me tested so I just got to keep my head up and continue on and give it to God. It sucks to think someone has read my journal, especially the folks in that office because they were often the main topics in my journal. Anyway, I am going to let go and let God.

Oh yeah, I also called Missy on my way to work and her brother has been missing for the past couple of days. She's worried because he had told her that niggaz was shooting at him for some reason. I told her I will pray for her brother. He ain't no thug though, so I don't see him getting too involved in a thug's affair to the point where someone would want to chop him down or even see him as a threat. Probably just chilling with some chick somewhere.

11:37 a.m. 9/21/04 The School of Education Lab
Today started kind of late because I was struggling this morning to shake the demons off my back. It has been a habit of mine to think my way out of things that involve intellect or unfavorable situations that can be manipulated to work in my favor, so this morning that's what my brain was trying to do. It was analyzing the situation with the school of graduate studies office either having seen my journal or having a copy of my journal and how I would extract the information. I tell you this brain of mine ain't no joke and it would not shut down easily. It wasn't the fact that I was worried; it was just that I wanted to know how it came about and who brought it about.

I had to get up and wash my face at about 8:30 this morning just to interrupt my thought process. My brain would not let it go easily, so even though I was still tired I couldn't sleep or fall back to sleep because my brain was too busy plotting. When I laid back down, I had a nice talk with God and eventually drifted back off into a light sleep. Yesterday I called Mrs. Hilling on my way to work (I'm not sure if I mentioned it) and she said she knew nothing about it and hadn't been invited to the party. Now I knew this was a lie because she's the only one that know Nia so I just let that be because she probably doesn't know what I know so she tried to play me like the rest of the snakes. I ain't tripping because I am the only one accountable here. I shouldn't have let something as valuable as this fall into the wrong hands. One down.

I called Chanel next. She met me after work and tried to act like she was the last one to see it and that she didn't read it, just opened it up to a page and saw her name. It just so happened that she opened it up to the page where I was talking about how she dropped the dime on me and how evil she was and how mad I was cause I had to come to work early because of her. She took it pretty well considering it was nothing that I hadn't told her to her face. She gave me the scoop and what I got from her was that the new guy who they hired, I guess after I left, had been given the assignment to go and clear space on the computer and print out anything that looked like it was needed for Hen Dog[18] to review. So I know about him now, and if I had thought about it the last time I went in the office to help a student out, he was sitting behind the desk with Ms. Wilming just a cheesing away. He had a sinister smirk on his face and came up to shake my hand and was very "friendly" as if he knew I was a real cat and

---

18 The School of Graduate Studies President's Administrative Assistant

a straight up player. It was as if he was congratulating me and I kind of wondered why he acted like he knew me so well because I had only helped him a couple of times. It was Satan staring me in the eye and I was so blind, I shook hands with the devil and didn't even know it.

After Chanel dropped me off back at the school, cause she wanted to show off her car that the married man bought her and gloat on some other things before I went to class, we talked about the situation. We had a group discussion and I think it is safe to say that the guy who irked me in class last time is not going to be a problem because he sees along with the other students and teacher that I am a straight up no-nonsense type of guy. I had to keep him focused and asked him to keep the comments to a minimum—of course in a professional and intellectual way—several times during our meeting which ran over because of him. Anyway, my presentation went well and everyone participated. I didn't just run my mouth and read to them like my peers. After that class, we had to wait in the hall for about half and a hour until our teacher showed up. She kind of looked like a hype, but we soon found out she is for real and a straight up tell-you-the-truth type of woman. You know she and I clicked.

We had a good class discussion on an article that was featured in the *Baltimore Sun* discussing the current state of schools and the choices they have to make because of the No Child Left Behind initiative by Bush. Basically it has created a billion-dollar industry for an educational software producer. Only thing was that she held class until like 9:15 because she enjoyed getting to know us and our personalities and we enjoyed getting to know her. I was just irked and anxious because Brother Dashings had called me and canceled our Monday night get together at Paul's house.

Jack called me wondering where I was at cause I told him about 7:15 and Paul called wondering the same. After class finally let out, I went and scooped Jack and I also called Brother Dashings again just to mess with him because I know he married and we sometimes forget that cause he so cool. On our way to Paul's I had to stop and get some gas cause I was sitting on (E)ddie, and I got 20 dollars out so we could order some pizza cause I hadn't eaten. When we got over there, boy what a surprise were we in for! Paul had a big screen TV with the surround sound and all of the extras that go along with it. It was actually a very nice and comfy bachelor's pad. Now I got a place to go instead of hanging with the knuckleheads.

Paul was a good host and was glad to have us. He had juice and soda, we ordered the pizzas, and he even had eating trays or tables so we were very comfortable and we made sure to mention several times that we appreciated his hospitality and that it was on from here on out.

Back to today. This morning I had a message from Missy saying her brother is missing again so I left her a message and let her know that the next time they get their hands on him to have him call me so I can give him some advice on the situation he's in. Which brings me to now: I hope I see the sister in church tonight with the problem so I can give her what the Spirit gave me. That will bring my heart some joy, or should I say some more joy.

This situation with my journal, although it was meant to bring me grief and worry, has actually brought me joy too because it lets me know I am on the right track and that God is allowing me to be sifted and tested to see if I can be shook. Thing is, this ain't shaking me. Satan has been trying, but it is only bringing me closer to God because who else can I run to when this world tries to persecute me wrongly? All I can say to those who are involved is get a life. I thank the Lord that He has exposed all of the snakes to me. I knew there were a couple, but He has exposed them all. Ms. Wilming said nothing to me when I came into that office the last time and I'm quite sure she knew. Looking back, that's probably why she had that sick look on her face when I came in and was smiling all up in my face. She didn't make a move to hug me or nothing. Had the roles been switched, I would have slipped off somewhere on my lunch break and called her. She has my celly number. Anyway, I ain't mad at her either. I just know.

Ok now for the scripture of the day: *For as the rain cometh down, and the snow from heaven, and returneth not thither, but watereth the earth, and maketh it bring forth and bud, that it may give seed to the sower, and bread to the eater: So shall my word be that goeth forth out of my mouth: it shall not return unto me void, but it shall accomplish that which I please, and it shall prosper in the thing whereto I sent it* (Isaiah 55:10-11). This is an encouraging verse and I think the key is that I have to make sure I am a sower of good seeds. I have to open my mouth and speak the truth and not just hold it, and I have to speak the truth through my lifestyle and not just be a Sunday morning only Christian. Very good verse!

The inspirational message for the day is: Letting Go of Urgency. Today I will peacefully approach one thing at a time. When in doubt, I will take first things first. I have the feeling that I haven't been studying for this LSAT the way I should and could if I really tried. At the same time though, from jump I have been telling myself that when the time comes I am not going to lean on my own understanding anyway because God has always seen me through. So I have been trying to be careful not to rely on my own ability by studying so much that when I do what I do, I won't be in danger of thanking or giving credit to myself and my studying abilities.

23

EMAIL EXCHANGE WITH NIA

6:01 p.m. 9/21/04 The Morgan View Lab
I knew drama was right around the corner and it came in the form of an email from Nia. Not really drama, just things that I would be concerned about. That's why it's important that I give it to God because I've been in a similar situation before where some of my emails to other girls were sent to my wifey. Those were outrageous hookup booty call type emails, so this too shall pass. This was Nia's response:

> *Whatever Charlie. Don't come at me with crap like that. Being a player yet you can throw scriptures and GOD around at will. I don't take that from you. I NEVER said that you DID have the money but I DID say that you always find ways to get what you want. Ask one of your girls for the money. Ask your parents, I mean. I don't care about the money. I already worked it out. And I don't care about whether you know how to keep your business to yourself or not cause I'm not there anymore, nor do I intend to come out that way for as long as I can think of. What I did care about was the fact that we were*

supposed to be, at least, friends. Friends are there for each other no matter what. If you had a prior commitment, that's understandable. However, if you wanted to see how I was doing (the fact that I could have been killed) and that this was also YOUR responsibility too, you could have at least come to see me. But nothing! You did nothing because you did not want to! If you wanted to, you would have, no matter what I said or how I acted toward you. So SCREW EVERYTHING ELSE! You lied about being a friend. You wanted me there for the sex, for going out and for keeping you from being lonely. That's all you wanted from me. But when it was time for you to step up and be a man, you backed out. I never asked anything from you. NEVER! The one time I needed you (life and death) you weren't there nor did you ever (even now) make an effort to be here for me. So screw friendship. I see we never had it!

Well chew on that for a while and I will be back to analyze and discuss after church cause she sent me another email too. I think she still wants to see me and I am going to call her while I wait for Brother Dashings.

9:55 p.m. 9/21/04 The Morgan View Lab
Today has been a full day. Men's study class was wonderful. We talked about some real important topics. Satan tried to work on me a bit because Brother Clay didn't want me to read because I always raise my hand and try to participate, but the Lord allowed me to quickly tell Satan to get behind me and put out of my mind that evil thought that he was hating on me and despising my youth. We talked about how we as Christian men should be ambassadors for Christ representing him to the fullest and how people in the world should say we are just like our daddy or should see Christ in us.

On the way to church, Brother Dashings and I had a very good conversation about how he prepares his sermons and I asked him if he had a copy of his last sermon and it just so happened that he did. We left early today for class because he had to do a Bible class with someone. I asked if there was a script that they used and he said yes. I asked if I could get a copy or see it and he said yes. When I saw his sermon I volunteered to type out his next sermon for him because he stated he really didn't like to type. I told him I'm typing all the time and I actually enjoy it now. When I looked at his sermon, I realized why when he preached the sermon it seemed as if he got lost a couple of times and was just reading to us because it was so small and cluttered with all types of information; it wasn't in the traditional outline format. If I had to teach by his script, it would be hard for me with 20/20 vision to look up and address the audience and still be able to glance down real quick and know where exactly I left off at.

I explained that if my typing didn't help his sermon go smooth the first time then he could tell me how he would like me to change it and I would do so accordingly. I told him if I am going to be his preaching assistant and apprentice that he has to use me. By him allowing me to type out his sermons, it may help him and take a burden off of him and it will also help me to get valuable practice and experience in taking what I want to say and turning it into a sermon. That was a very valuable conversation to me because it will help me in the future to save some souls and hide a multitude of sins (James 5:20).

Class went well and I shook Satan off my back, and it was encouraging to know that some of the same people that are there every week are being sifted and persecuted for trying to do right also. After class Satan was really mad because Brother Clay asked for a volunteer to close us out in prayer and one of the brothers who always volunteers volunteered and Brother Clay told him, like he told me, you always volunteer. Then he looked my way and of course I made eye-to-eye contact and he must have seen the hunger. God is good because He really just gives me words and soaks me with His Spirit to the point where people know I can't even fake the front, and He has truly been good to me.

I couldn't recap what I said if I tried, but I will tell you this: It moved every man in that room and when I opened my eyes, just like last time, the brothers were looking at me in a completely different way. All glory to God! He really gives me strength and confidence because He allows not only myself but others to know and realize that He speaks through me. After the prayer, brothers were hugging me talking bout I got everybody fooled like I don't really know the Lord, and "What's up, prayer warrior?" Every comment was out of love and was a genuine compliment to my praying ability tonight and the talent which God has given me.

After church I did my usual fellowshipping and gave my love to everybody then I went in the preacher's quarters where Brother Dashings was. I asked him about the script and he showed me, after me and Brother Bethem jokingly got on him for a minute. Afterwards he showed me the script and he thought I was just loud talking him in front of Brother Clay and Brother Bethem, but he realized that wasn't the case when Brother Clay told him that I was talking him up in class and praising him for being an example to me. He realized I wasn't trying to front because I had asked for the script in the car. As we were leaving, Brother Bethem challenged me to learn the script so I can teach others and I told him cool. He then said I'm going to see if you gone be here and stand up. I told him I am going to let my works speak for themselves because he said something about coming to church on Sunday evening and during the week.

My past record for the past couple of months or since I linked up with Brother Dashings has been a testament to my newfound commitment. I love a challenge and I need to be challenged because it motivates me to do my best, so I am off and running. Tomorrow I look forward to teaching the young bucks' class and that should be very enjoyable. The next thing on my agenda is addressing this Nia issue because she sent me another email. I called her and left a message but she didn't pick up. Well to address the above notes, I think they are self-explanatory and that was my brain trying to make everything cool.

After today's class I realized when you trying to do right, everything ain't gone be cool. It's going to be a lot of drama and I have to expect it and accept it with joy and love. The best way to conquer evil is with good and with love—by loving my enemies, doing them right and praying for them. I will drop a heap of coals upon their head. She is not my enemy, but I am going to kill the evil with love. I ain't perfect and in the beginning I stated that. I am a hot mess just like anyone else who is honest with themselves. Thank the Lord for His grace and mercy.

24

FINAL RESPONSE TO NIA

12:57 p.m. 9/22/04 The Morgan View Lab
Yesterday has come and gone and today is just arriving. Last night I had a good night's sleep because my conscience was clear and my spirit renewed. I slept this morning good and late. God is good! I got up in the Spirit, hopped in the shower and decided to throw on my Milwaukee Brewers throwback with GoodGame and the number 6 on the back. As I left this morning the song "If Heaven's Not My Home" was prevalent on my mind for some reason. I haven't heard it sang in a while, but I think that was the Spirit giving me something to meditate on. As I left my house I also remembered that Mom said my box should be here this morning, so I went to the post office and sure enough it had arrived. I went back to the room and opened it up and immediately started laughing because I thought they were playing a practical joke or messing with me. On top was a white dress shirt that looked like it would fit CJ (and I thought they had put it in there for padding because it had a huge musty yellow ring around the armpits).

I thought Charlene was being the trout that she can be at times. Earlier during the week she had gassed me and told me she had gotten me a button-up, so when I opened that box I hit the floor and started rolling. Mom hooked me up with the tapes of the young brother who was a preacher and a Walkman to play them in. That is going to help me tremendously. She also hooked me up with $100 and a bad mamma jamma black pinstripe suit coat so now I am forced to step my dress game up. At the bottom was another one of Charlene's "button-ups."

On the way to work I called Charlene, but she didn't answer so I called Mom and asked about the shirts and they were actually serious! Mom thought I was being ungrateful by talking about the shirts, but they were so small I just knew that Charlene was trying to be funny. I didn't even have to try them on to know that the arms weren't going to meet my wrist. I kept it real and had jokes about them, but I did say thank you and showed my appreciation for the other things. I guess later I am going to have to call back and say thank you again because I think they really looked at it as me being ungrateful, but I am so amazed that Mom or even Charlene would think that I am that small. LOL it's all good though.

I checked my email and I got no response from Nia. I tried to call her last night again but to no avail. On a more positive note, Sandra (the new tenant) and I talked last night until about 1:40. I was trying to leave but the Spirit told me to stay there because we were talking about spiritual things and the word of God. She ended up opening up to me about how she was depressed not too long ago then she finally gave up and asked God for help and things started coming together. I had just got back from church and hadn't eaten or even went to my room yet, so I wanted to leave. Out of the time I spent there though she told me that she wanted to go to church with me, so that is good. The conversation kicked off because she heard me on the phone to Missy talking about how Satan's been on my heels since I've been trying to do right and I had to struggle to keep the monkey off my back.

Oh yeah, I forgot to mention that yesterday I sat down before I took my nap and did a complete mini-diagnostic LSAT test and I got only 2 or 3 more than half of the answers right and that don't equal Harvard, so I gots to keep studying, practicing and praying. Anyway, I didn't get an email back from Nia so everything is going good.

So now let's get the scripture of the day: *The centurion answered and said, Lord, I am not worthy that thou shouldest come under my roof:*

but speak the word only, and my servant shall be healed (Matthew 8:8). This is a reminder of the humbleness that I should also exude. The man was exactly right. I am not worthy, and none of us are worthy. The inspirational message of the day is Trusting Ourselves. Today, God . . . help me to let go of shame-based rigid rules. I will choose the freedom of loving, listening and trusting. That's a wrap.

10:25 p.m. 9/22/04 The Morgan View Lab

Tonight has been another blessed and wonderful night and today has been wonderfully blessed also. No drama and no mess. I guess that means I better be prepared cause Satan is preparing his strategy or approach to come at me three times worse than he came at me before. I think and I am careful when I say this that I am getting stronger in my weak areas by the grace of God. I thank the Lord that He has allowed me to separate from the people, places and things that I used to associate with before. I better be careful though because I did tell Sherman Merman that I would come see her tonight and drop off her DVDs. I watched one last night that was actually pretty good with Lark Voorhies, the girl who played Lisa in *Saved by the Bell*.

Tonight in church I was in the youth class helping to teach and that was an exhausting affair because the young men today are difficult just for the sake of being difficult or to appear cool. Nowadays, just like it was when I was younger, it's cool to not go along with the regularly scheduled program. Brother Baffum and I were arming them with scriptures to teach others why we do the things we do and that there is only one church built by Christ. I listened to a couple of the tapes that Mom sent me and they were exactly right; that brother don't hold no punches and he tells it like it is. He also is wise beyond his years and the Lord has revealed a lot to him. He is showing me why it is so important that I stop playing and go ahead and do what I was called to do, because people will know that the things I speak come from God if I speak it while I still have my youth. That brother sounds like he's 40 years old and has knowledge that the average person our age has no clue about. I am happy to say that he has found himself and the truth.

After church I showed my love to everyone then me and Brother Dashings took off. We had a good discussion on the young brother's preaching, the power of God, sin and sex. He has to speak about sex on Saturday at the men's prayer breakfast. I called Nia again and she didn't pick up, so I am through calling until she responds. She really has me confused and I am so glad that the Lord has given me other matters to think about and focus on because if he hadn't this thing would be bugging me.

I tried to skip the middleman by calling but that hasn't worked so I am just going to leave that situation alone. Let it go and let God. On another note, I called and spoke with Missy. Her birthday is Monday which is also Tweety's birthday so I am going to have to remember to call Mom because that's when she goes through her thangs and I don't blame her. I am going to create more study sheets with scriptures on them. Hopefully, they will inspire me to open my mouth and tell others how good God is because He truly has smiled on me.

Oh yeah, Brother Dashings and I stopped by Popeye's to get some food and the lady at the counter recognized me, so that was kind of cool. Brother Dashings also allowed me to use the study guide he and Brother Bethem use to teach people about why they should be baptized so I can get the verses and questions for myself and adapt it to the way I talk and the way I would teach someone. I am going to edit this letter to Oprah for Mom so she can send it off for Tiny to get cosmetic surgery. Well I guess that is it for now. I'll holla.

25

SUNSHINE GOES TO FIGHT NIGHT

1:01 p.m. 9/24/04 The Morgan View Lab
All things considered, so far this has been a good week and today has started off well. I actually woke up this morning earlier than I thought I would, because my active night life kept me up longer than I wanted to be (as usual). I ended up getting dressed last night for nothing, walking down to Herb's crib and doing nothing, but as of now I see the purpose. It helped keep Jack busy and kept him from smoking any weed. That is a good thing and he was definitely feenin last night, but when it was all said and done he had his first sober night in a long time. When we went back, Herb was in the basement playing X-Men and I am really through just playing games with grown men because that is not something you do everyday. So instead of going down there in a smoke-filled room getting my clothes filled with smoke, we sat on the porch and talked about the struggle and how good God has been to us.

We ended up walking across the street to the liquor store since we didn't go out as a time killer. I got a Smirnoff Ice and he got a Black and Mild. Of course that wasn't his drug of choice (the Smirnoff wasn't my drug of choice either though). Anyway, we sat and talked and chilled for a minute before we made up our mind that we weren't going to just sit there. Hindsight is always 20/20 and that was one of the things we talked about. Since I hadn't went out in such a long time or at least it seems, I allowed my hopes and expectations to be high on man, and God used that to teach me. Once again, I ain't missing nothing. The world is passing my old associates by and I'm steady growing.

I got up earlier than I thought I would because last night Missy called and told me she was going to give me her address so I could send her a card. That was on my mind this morning and that's what motivated me to get up, get dressed and go to the bookstore. I did that and I also got a mechanical pencil, white out and a Donald Goines Book.

No drama so far and I still haven't smoked anything. As Jack and I were talking last night, I realized that Sunday will be my two-month anniversary. God is good! I can do all things through Christ who strengthens me. The next major victory is victory over the lust of the flesh. I am going to begin a vicious prayer attack on it real soon, Lord's will. I plan on finishing this entry up then going to the room to do a couple of practice tests and listen to another Brother Preston tape. Last night, Jack and I listened to the sermon about the Samaritan woman and the well, and Jack agreed with me that that brother is cold. I also forgot that Brother Clint called me after coming from the bookstore and asked if I could help form a crew of brothers to go to the church and setup tables for tomorrow's prayer breakfast.

Z, Jack's girl, just called me and asked where Jack is at. I spoke with her a brief moment and helped her to get her mind right. God is really revealing to me that a lot of the people I know or see or come in contact with need His help and I can be the one to help bring them to Him and give them peace. That's all that most want is peace and to be able to feel content. So the work is plenty like the Bible says, the laborers are few though (Luke 10:2; Matthew 9:37). On that note, the scripture of the day is: *Fear not; I am the first and the last: I am he that liveth, and was dead; and, behold, I am alive for evermore, Amen; and have the keys of hell and of death* (Revelation 1:17-18). That is a powerful scripture and it helps to solidify my faith and remind me that I serve a mighty God. The inspirational theme of the day is Allowing Ourselves to be Needy. Today I will accept my needs and my needy side. I believe I deserve to get my needs met, and I will allow that to happen.

11:19 p.m. 10/3/04 The Morgan View Lab
This morning I woke up and shook Satan off my back because last night I had the best sleep that I've had in days. I didn't even sleep as good as I slept last night in the plush hotel in DC. I wanted so bad to stay in the bed and sleep until the last minute so I wouldn't have to serve during worship, then the Spirit called to my remembrance that this was the first Sunday that we were going to have two services, so I was needed. I hopped out of bed and got my mind right quick, hopped in the shower and had a nice talk with my Father. Last night He kept me from fornicating because after I left the game, Randy gave me a ride home in the Acura and I was feeling some kind of way. It was like just from riding in luxury and Mr.Good-Game was ready to come out.

After the game I came to the room and listened to some gospel music for a hot minute then Sunshine called. I don't know if I ever mentioned Mrs. Sunshine, but she is an associate of Violet's. She also is a graduate student going after her MBA, from a suburb on the outskirts of Philly. She is light skinned with a JLO booty so most dudes would be thirsting just to even taste liquid from her fountain. Me on the other hand, I've always dogged her and talked about the few hairs she got on her lip like she got a full-grown mustache. I don't give her a break. While I was at the game I called her to get some bootleg movies from her cause her dad be having them by the boatload. I forgot that there was a fight going on so when she called, I invited her to go to Brother Dashings with me. The original plan was for her to come over to my crib and we were going to "watch a DVD."

When I called her though I had other things in mind and I believe she was down. So when I set the invitation out there, she accepted and I felt that for some reason she still wanted to kick it with me cause she was down no matter what we did or where we went. That kind of touched me cause I ain't did nothing but be a jerk to her for the most part. I know now though that she like the fact that I don't sweat her like the rest of these niggas out here. Thing is though, she's definitely sweatable.

Anyway, she volunteered to drive over to Brother Dashings and that was real cool. So it was just us and Brother Dashings watching the fight. Oh and what a fight it was! Boy Mayorga and Felix Trinidad slugged it out for eight rounds. Trinidad was a better, more trained fighter so he got the best of Mayorga, but Mayorga showed he was a straight up man with a heart as big as Nicaragua, his country home. Felix put a beat down on the dude, but he never backed down and kept coming. The dude is straight up crazy, but his craziness made it a good fight.

Mrs. Sunshine is a self-proclaimed "artsy fartsy" chick and that's the type of guys she like so how I got in the mix, I don't know but I am in. I say I am in cause that was only her second time watching boxing and she thinks it is barbaric. Not once did she complain though and she even involved herself in the conversations and had something to say about the fighters. She brought the woman's opinion to the fight which was appreciated. I also appreciated her not tripping and not calling me out for not being the exemplary Christian that I should be. After the fight I invited her up but she declined cause she was sleepy.

We ended up talking for a while in her car about different aspects of life and she told me about her current situation as far as relationships go. She had the dude she wanted to get married to but she ain't told him. She been with him a long time off and on, but he don't know the love she got for him cause she won't tell him. How dumb is that? She then went on to tell me that she only have sex with one person at a time and she had someone else she is having sex with at the time.

When she told me that, I just hopped out her truck and dipped. She hollered for me to come back but I just kept walking cause I can't really respect that. We were both feeling each other (and at least to me it felt like we were building something) and it was clear from the way she said it that the one person she was having sex with wasn't her man. I could've turned around and heard her out, but at that point it felt like a waste of time. I wasn't in the mood to try and persuade her that I should be the one she should be giving it to. It's just not in my DNA to hate on someone else, and persuading her seemed like I would've had to talk down about her other dude and lift myself up.

I went to bed and dodged trouble last night. God is good! Back to today, I made it to church early and even got an assignment. Although I wasn't obligated, I volunteered. I owe the Lord my service. After church I showed everybody my love and as I was getting ready to leave, Young Arnold asked me for a ride to the crib cause his mother was staying at church for song rehearsal. I told him he could ride with me before I asked him how far he live like a dummy. He was so scared of my driving and we talked about it. It was because he's been in several accidents where he saw it was coming but was quiet cause he thought the drivers saw what was up too. He told me after like the fourth accident, he learned not to keep his mouth shut and to speak up.

Anyway, he stayed a good distance from the church and when we got there we passed up his crib and went to Pizza Hut. We killed the pizza, watched some football and eventually fell out from the itis. I set my alarm on my phone and it woke me up for church and I was reluctant but I knew I had to be an example. Arnold let me know he wasn't going back and that was kind of discouraging, but I got on my mission by myself. I was so tired and Satan was in my ear. I was heading back to the crib, but the Lord spoke to me and told me to take my tail back to church, so that is exactly what I did. The Spirit was actually guiding the wheel for me because I was tired and the nap had only teased me and pissed me off that I couldn't finish it. So my spirit wasn't the best when I got to church although I was thankful and had realized that the Lord brought me back (and on time).

I even volunteered myself somehow, before I realized what I had said, to serve during evening worship too. Brother Clint preached and he's getting somewhat better although his sermons are better geared toward nonbelievers and visitors, and it wasn't any of either there. I did my duty and showed my love and came home. Brother Clint spoke the message, but it really didn't inspire or prick me; that's why I say I did my duty. I did sing and pray in spirit and truth and I truly gave thanks to God for bringing me but at the same time I was fighting Satan in my mind telling me that I was sleepy.

After church I came home and took a nap cause I still got to watch that boring video for class tomorrow. I think I am just going to fast forward to all of the notes and just write the notes down. Sandra came through and confided in me that we have a similar problem and that is controlling our sexual urges. I gave her some scripture and since she came to my room, I was armed and very dangerous. The scriptures on my wall came in real handy because they had the general scriptures that help me, so I shared them with her and I can tell she got mad respect for a nigga now. I challenged her to stand up for what she believes and the scripture woke me up out of my slumber to do His will cause I heard someone knocking at the door while I was sleeping but I ignored it cause I wanted my full three-hour nap. She called me though twice and I had to get up when she said it was something spiritual that she wanted to talk about. So we ended up talking about some deep stuff and I armed her with some things and told her to read up on Paul. She got locked out her room too, so I left her my key and told her she could chill in my room until she finds her roommate. I could go into more detail but I am tired and still got work to do so I gots to keep it moving. I got a big day tomorrow, so I will holla later.

26

MR.GOODGAME OFF THE ROPES

11:33 a.m. 10/18/04 The School of Education Lab

God is good and treats me better than I treat myself. What a week I just came out of! The Lord pulled me through and allowed me to come out of it praising Him. I went through a storm and my faith and patience were tried. My patience was because I was putting myself in some compromising positions and turning back to the beggarly elements that God pulled me from and I had to have patience with myself to know that sooner or later I was going to wisen up and stop being drawn into foolishness. I stayed at Herb's house this week where it ain't nothing but smoking, drinking and foul play. I was right up in the mix and my dumb tail was quenching the Spirit. I wasn't drawing. I was being drawn and I actually had a slight urge to hit a nasty Black and Mild one night. I also ended up fornicating with a chick which I have no love for and really don't particularly feel because she is lazy in bed. That was because I let Satan steal my joy and I had a lonely spirit overtake me this past week.

I am back now though. My faith was tried and tested because it seemed as if I was falling back into the ditch which God had pulled me out of. But my faith in God told me He wouldn't let me fall and that He would bring me through the storm. Satan tried to reinitiate the Spirit of depression in me. Before I started this journal I used to think I was bipolar because one minute I would be on top of the world—King Dingaling PimpTight Mr.Good-Game—and the next minute I would be searching for someone to validate my existence or looking for some female to be with to make me feel better or should I say feel good about myself. Through it all God was with me and everything happens for a reason, so I count it all joy that I could go through that experience. I didn't get a chance to enter any entries this weekend because my mind was not where it needed to be and I didn't redeem the time.

I spent most of Saturday at PK and Randy's crib kicking butt in NBA Live 2005. Ever since I stopped smoking I been dominating the game circuit among my peers. It was my first time playing the new Live and I was spanking fools. Speaking of fools, the Lord was with me for real because I ended up going on a dope run with my guy PK to drop some purple haze off to one of his customers. He didn't tell me that at first and I wasn't paying attention til it was too late and I was in the car. While we were at his house, he asked me if I wanted to ride with him somewhere. At first I told him no, but they had been smoking so much I had the munchies and my stomach started talking to me so I was like I'll ride if you will take me to grab something to eat. He was like cool. Now that I look back, the nigga was just scary and didn't want to go by himself and leave me and/or Loban at the crib by ourselves.

We ended up waiting in a gas station, hot as a firecracker for like 20-25 minutes, three deep in a totally tinted out Acura—even the front windows were tinted on a car full of dope. I told PK he's a good dude because I know I wouldn't be waiting nowhere that long in a hot car riding dirty for nobody when I've driven halfway across town to meet you and you ain't there. While sitting in the car, I begin to realize how good God is, cause I was telling that fool PK he had us out there bad but he was only concerned about making that quick 25 dollars. So that was another instance that made me realize that God was looking out for me.

Sunday morning and Sunday evening I went to church. I also did the closing prayer Sunday morning. I don't know why but I tried to keep it simple and sweet so it went kind of fast, but I did get all my thoughts in there. It was a humbling experience because usually when I pray all kinds of people come up to me and are surprised at how intimate my prayers are as if I can't talk to God like I know Him. Anyway, the Lord brought me through a lot and He is still good!

I also got my workout on this weekend too. Sheila called me back and we had a nice conversation, ironed things out, and I spoke with Missy and Quin. Missy is starting to become something like a bug-a-boo and some of her attempts at being manipulative are being exposed cause she's not good at it. She has been working Mom cause she can't work me. Quin is supposed to buy a ticket to come up here and I'm supposed to reimburse her with half. I don't mind cause she's done a lot for me.

I borrowed Randy's Fight Night and last night Jack had an incident with his girl Z at the church so I scooped him and took him with me for a while. I got him something to eat, gave him some t-shirts, then we went to Herb's to put a bug in the ear of one of the brothers that was coming to church but all of a sudden stopped. I told him I would like to see him when he got a chance and I left it at that, and I also let him know we missed him. The crazy thing is that he is the boyfriend of the preacher's daughter and she just had a baby not two weeks ago. Ever since she had the baby

I have been seeing him at Herb's, but I never saw him over there before then. It has me perplexed but I wanna try and get him back in the church, even if he is smoking. I'm going to pray for the brother and leave that to the Spirit.

This morning the Spirit woke me up before my alarm clock went off and for that I am thankful. I forgot to mention that I did repent for my sins, especially the fornication in front of the church, and I asked them to pray for me that I may seize the opportunity to talk about God and plant a seed. It worked cause that night I talked to Jack about smoking cigarettes on the church grounds and the brother at Herb's house.

The inspirational theme for the day is Throwing Out the Rule Book. Today I will stop clinging to the painful lessons of the past and open myself to the positive lessons today and tomorrow hold for me. I trust that I can and will take care of myself now. I trust that the plan is good, even when I don't know what it is. The scripture of the day is: *And he that overcometh, and keepeth my works unto the end, to him will I give power over the nations* (Revelation 2:26). Powerful stuff! I'm trying to be one of them! It's a wrap cause I got the boring night classes tonight and I wanna get some sleep so I can watch Monday Night Football.

27

DRAMA, DRAMA, DRAMA, AND AN LSAT SCORE

12:48 p.m. 10/26/04 Home Computer in the Mill

Well I made it back safely by the wonderful grace of God. It was a mission getting out of Baltimore and the Lord showed me one more revelation, gave me one more warning and allowed me to see things a little bit clearer before I left. P called me at about 5:30 p.m. all hysterical talking about come get him cause they were about to tow his car cause he was stopped by the police for riding with no seatbelt and a suspended license. To make a long story short, my heart went out to the nigga cause he sounded like a lil scared itch and I could tell he was shook so Loban and I hopped in the truck and went to save the chump. We ended up getting lost for about an hour trying to get to the fool and got there right after the tow truck did.

The only reason they didn't tow it was because Loban and I know how to deal with cops and spoke in a humble manner as we approached while P sat on the hood of his car looking dusted and disgusted, scowling at the cops for doing their job. By the time we finally got the nigga, it was time for me to go to the airport, but I asked P to take me and he got slick at the mouth and made me call him a hoe ass nigga. The thing is I meant it and I've known for quite some time that he is, but for some reason the nigga keeps ending up in my circle due to a lack of friends I guess. The Lord showed me before I left though that he is one nigga I don't need to have any love for cause he is like a virus. When I get back I am going to try my best to avoid this nigga like the plague and when the time is right let him know he got more itch-like tendencies than most chicks I know.

Well anyway, I made it to the airport right on time and had a nice trip. Side note, Dr. Tailor and I hand delivered the finished version of the design to Adler Displays a couple hours before I left then went to Pizza Hut and ate. She also took me to pick up my crab cakes to bring home to my mom. When I got here, Charlene was late but she brought Charity with her. It ain't nothing like family! Last night we watched *The Johnson Family Reunion* and got our laugh on.

Oh and I almost forgot! The reason that I really wanted to make sure I got a journal entry in today was because last night I looked at my LSAT test scores for the first time with the family and I got a 156. The average score is 150 and I am only in the 69th percentile. I am kind of disappointed, but I have faith and trust God's plan. If it's not meant to be, then it won't be. My score is probably good enough to get into a rankadank law school, but I am not exactly sure that is what I want to do. I asked God to guide the way. I am not sure, but I think a low score means to go another direction. Most of the law schools I was looking at are asking for at least a 160. We will see though. I am not satisfied in the least bit with my score because I really feel I put the effort forward, but that's life.

Anyway, now I am reading *Whoreson* by Donald Goines and I really see a lot of myself in this young man but I don't know where it came from. For some reason I read people and been reading people's most subtle reactions in the same way that he describes for quite some time now. If I didn't have this consciousness from God that I have, I would be the best pimp that I ever met in my life. I haven't met another cat yet that goes harder than me and is as real. Anyway, I am going to get back to my book and we will see how the law school thing develops as the weeks develop.

11:50 p.m. 11/1/04 Dr. Tailor's Office

God is good! I made it back to Baltimore safely and He allowed me to leave just in time, because I was losing focus. This trip reminded me why the

Lord has sent me on the journey I am currently on. I was becoming very bitter and pissed at my father and my brother because neither respects Mom but expects her to give them the world. Vick has completely lost his marbles and the hate and bitterness that he holds inside for Mom has totally consumed him and his spirit. He's so full of Satan that he doesn't even listen to knowledge or wisdom anymore. Pops so used to Mom being a superwoman that he doesn't even appreciate her or talk to her with respect. You reap what you sow though, and both him and Vick are going to need the family before it is all over and done with. Mom had to remind me to love them in spite of and she really had to talk to me because at one point or another I wanted to go upside both of their heads.

Mom asked me one morning to clean out the attic because the city had placed an empty dumpster in front of our house. She wanted to call Vick, even though she knew she was going to hear it. I warned her that it was early. When he finally made it over, he raised hell and was cussing Mom out in front of the nephews. The more Mom tried to calm him down, the more ignorant and disrespectful he became. He only cared about making his point which was that she woke him up early in the morning to clean an attic which he had got kicked out of earlier. Still holding on to the bitterness and hate from the past.

We finally got in the attic and I had to keep Mom from jumping on the fool cause he would not just shut up and work. He had to keep fussing just like Dad. Mom left for work and that fool still was talking and the funny part was when I'd point out the error in his arguments, he would say he didn't say that and acted as if I was twisting his words. I lost it and told him to stop f'ing talking to me because he was whining like a lil B.I. and that he was so gone he didn't even know what he be saying. I think it hurt him, but he still didn't shut up. Before it was all over and done with, I had to tell him to move around before we be fighting. That evil spirit of his took me there, cause he don't listen to sensibility or wisdom. He's not content til you get on the same ignorant and foolish level with him then he starts to hear and pay attention. That's a doggone shame and it hurt me afterwards that I had to let loose on him like that but that's what he enjoys. Satan has him feeling like he's not a part of the family, that we kicked him out, but the thing is, that fool chose his path just like the rest of us. To this day, he chooses to separate himself from the family because he can't smoke in Mom's house and that's all he really wants to do in life.

Dad, on the other hand, hadn't paid Mom Charity's child support for the month and Mom actually was very lenient over the years because she never once filed papers on that fool while we were in Mississippi. I hate to say it but my pops is a bum and he has not shown me how to be a father at all. It's probably the reason why I've forced several abortions and run from a relationship that involves the possibility that I might be the dad because I am afraid I won't be a good dad yet. I just pray that the Lord have mercy on my soul.

The day I left, I saw myself in Pops and it hurt me so. It literally pricked my heart because he gave Mom 150 of the 200 dollar child support that he supposed to give her every month, and he gave it to her on the day I left which just so happened to be the last freaking day of the month. So you know Mom struggled the whole month. He expected Mom to buy 50 dollar brakes for the blue Corsica out of the lil money that he gave her which was already 50 dollars short. We were leaving for church when Mom sent him to get the brakes and he came back cause they weren't open yet and gave Mom like 100 dollars. When Mom asked him where the rest of her change was, he told her to shut up and gone like she was some chick on the street. What made it so bad is that he acted as if she owed it to him and was sweating him for something that she knew she shouldn't have asked for cause it was rightfully his.

I do the same thing and have the same arrogant attitude with some of the chicks I deal with. I just take and rape them for their belongings, especially money. When I say rape I don't mean rape in the literal sense but speaking metaphorically. I rape them for their goods. I really started to feel bad about that because I can see you doing that to some woman on the street but to do it to your wife? If I don't change when I get married, I may send my wife through hell.

Speaking of wife, I called Lala because for some reason I missed her and was wondering how she was doing a lot. Even though the night before I called her I hooked up with this Mexican chick that I used to talk to back in the day when I was working at the school of graduate studies. We talked while I was at work on IM. I actually hit it and it was decent. She has a nice lil spot, is about to get her masters, is a high school teacher, and has everything going for her like Lala. I hit it the first night though and have not built any love for this young woman. I just created an attraction by being my cocky and funny self and she just eventually made up in her mind on the strength that I am a real dude. I wasn't trying to do too much and I wasn't pressed because I had also seen a chick I'd met on BlackPlanet earlier that night and met her at O'Danny's for a couple of two dollar long island ice teas. She was supposed to call me before she headed back out to the 'burbs.

Back to Lala. She agreed to meet me and I really didn't have to put up a fight. We went to the lakefront and talked. I was me and wasn't trying to do too much, but I was my usual cocky and funny self and I could tell that she was happy that we hooked back up. I wasn't pressed for her either because I had some nookie the night before, but I did want to kiss her because I missed her and was happy to see her. I know I love this girl because she makes my heart smile. I really be cheesing on the inside every time I can crack her hard exterior and get her to laugh.

We ended up having a nice talk but it was like it used to be with me doing most of the talking and her listening because she says she doesn't trust me. I always used to say that talking to her was like pulling teeth. She didn't seem bitter or angry and before it was all over with I think I had reached back in to her spirit and opened her heart to me. I had to let her know though that I wasn't trying to get back in her life, but I did remind her about our pact that we made before we broke up: we would find each other in '06 to see how we had grown.

I asked her some crucial questions like why she came to see me and who she had had sex with after I left. She answered the first with an "I don't know" and the second with the fact that she had been celibate. That was the first crack. I started smiling because I knew then that she truly loves me (notice not loved) in her own way and still cares for me. I began picking at my faults in a jokingly cocky way and asked her what was so bad about me. The conversation just flowed from there. A park ranger drove by and said the park was closed, so we left and went to Pops crib so she could drop me off. Somewhere in there I asked for a kiss and she wasn't sure so I didn't press her. I let her go cause I had really enjoyed myself with her and felt on top of the world because my conscience felt clear concerning her and our relationship.

About 10 minutes later she called me and asked me what if she'd changed her mind. I told her that it was her prerogative and she had the right. I didn't ask what she was referring to cause I really wasn't pressed. She had to come out and say, "What if I changed my mind about kissing you, idiot?" I was still like well that's your prerogative still. You can meet me at my dad house in five minutes. So she came and I got in her car and kissed her lightly on the lips. It was really just a tease cause I pulled away and invited her inside. We went upstairs and talked for a while and watched *Elimidate* and *Cheaters* before I asked for another kiss. She was playing hard to get so I let her then asked if she was ready to leave. She pretended like she was and when I led her to the door, she turned around, closed the door and began to kiss me. These kisses became passionate but I broke it off showing some self-control and told her it was time to go.

Then came the slammer. She asked, "What if I don't want to go and what if I want to do something else?" I tried to discourage her by stopping her from kissing me like three times and asking if she was sure she wanted to do this, and that just seemed to help her make up her mind even more to go all the way. I didn't want that on my conscience and she doesn't know it but she has control over my emotions because I love her and I don't want to get tied up with that love feeling for a good long while because it is a major weakness. I finally got her to stop and think about it but we went back to kissing. This time she stopped and said, "I'm sorry but I got to go." I told her don't be sorry. "I'm glad you're finally using your head cause I don't want you to do something that you might regret." I could tell that she wanted to, but my messages were hitting home and killing the mood.

I love her so much that I would have been right back entangled in her and all the drama that I would bring to her 'cause I am still not a one-woman man yet. So I didn't want to bring her back into that. I'd rather just have friendship than hurt her. I was proud of myself for sparing both our feelings and hearts. Oh, but the drama came the next day because during our conversation at the lake front trying to be funny I asked her if she had gotten any crazy emails since I had left and she told me no cause she doesn't check that account anymore. Well just my luck she checked it the next day and discovered that she had been forwarded my email thread with Nia about the abortion.

How crazy is that? Drama, drama and more drama! I don't think it's a coincidence cause it shows that she received it that night! What am I to do? Absolutely nothing cause although it shows that it came from my account, I know I didn't send it. It would profit me nothing for her to know that, so I really just let her know that I didn't send it. Yeah, a chick said she was pregnant by me, but I wasn't sure and yeah she was in the same position you were, hurt. She really snapped on me and was hurt cause someone had went through what she went through and I put her there. Eventually she called and apologized for being so harsh and I think that was on the account of one of my girl cousins being in her ear, but I didn't see her again before I left so I am not sure what is up with that situation. I think if I try too hard to figure out how she got the email or try to let her know what happened with the situation, it'll just create more mess so I am going to go with the philosophy that more is less and less is more.

Well, enough about that. Charity got a job at a Taste of Philly and I had to go pick her up twice. I am so proud of her; she really is growing up to be a fine young lady. My nephews got a taste of the disciplinary uncle and I think I instilled a little respect in each one of their hearts. I went to pick Fat Mack up from school one day and he was disobeying the teacher right in front of my face, so I took him home and starved him and helped him with his homework. The next day Fat Mack did good but Billy was in the hallway for disrespecting the teacher so I took him home and beat him all across his head and hands. He probably think his uncle is crazy cause I got loose on him but that was what he needed. CJ wasn't really a problem. He loves to learn and I am so proud of him; I just had to touch him up a lil bit.

Overall, the trip was wonderful and I didn't even come close to smoking so the four month anniversary passed without any conflict. Well I think that is a wrap for today. I am going to get started on these law school applications even though I am planning on taking a year off to work after school. I'm also going to be preparing my resume. I'll holla.

28

TOO CLOSE TO HOME

11:31 p.m. 11/8/04 Dr. Tailor's Office
Today God has given me another opportunity which I didn't earn to get right with Him and redeem the time. I got up and made it to work kind of early because Satan was trying to control my thoughts. Not just sneak in, he was trying to control them. I had to get up out the bed and make it to the shower so I could get right with God. Just that lil talk helps so much. Last night I had a dream about Lala and I getting back together and me marrying her and finally having the family that we should have had years ago.

All week I was whooping Satan round after round and then Saturday evening I took an L. I drove to McD's to get something to eat after being in the lab for most of the day. For some crazy reason, I went to Herb's house to eat. Temptation to see what was going on sucked me over there and kept me over there all night. We ended up going over to the Haven and they bought me a couple of rounds. An old drunk guy kept coming over trying to hang with us, so I talked him into buying all of us a round of drinks, which he did. It's almost as if I was trying to show them clowns one more time that the boy got a million-dollar mouthpiece. When I do get right, it will be a legacy out there about yo boy. Hopefully that will cause more people to take a closer look at God 'cause I will have done a 180.

I felt guilty Sunday morning until I got in the shower and spoke with God. I was really down on myself then I thought about the scripture that said a righteous man falleth seven times and gets up seven times, and that helped my spirit to go to church and worship Him in spirit and truth. It felt good to see all of my church family and I saw Dashings's wife. She said she had a plate for me earlier in the week so that made me feel good. Brother Dashings is really a big help. He is a realist like me and it just feels good to be honest and feel honesty from someone who ain't my immediate family cause I find myself dealing with snakes due to a lack of company.

Sunday evening I went back to church and when I got home I watched *Arthur* and *Ray* on bootleg. *Ray* was good but *Arthur* is another attempt by the white man to rewrite and twist history to make a fictional character seem real, which leads to today. When I got to work, I checked my emails first. Boy, was I in for a surprise. It is pure

D hell at home. Mom and Charlene are trying to stand up for Jesus, but I feel like they need me to help give them that extra push to make it up the hill. Sometimes I wonder why our family has to go through so much hell when we try so hard to be Christ-like but that is almost like an oxymoron. I just have to pray for them cause my heart is heavy thinking of all the hell that Satan is causing in their life through Pops and Vick's trifling tails. It almost makes me want to tell them to leave them niggaz behind and move somewhere else; leave them bums to fend for themselves.

But no Christ would not do that. I don't think God would have that cup removed from them but my heart goes out to them cause I know it is not easy to bear and that is probably why I left. Matter of fact ain't no probably to it. That is why I left. I have a whole lot more selfishness in me than they do. That's why I can just dip on my family cause Charlie C is my pops and I am a junior and I have a lot of my pops ways, but I am trying to separate myself from all negative actions, feelings and thoughts. Pray for me. I responded to Charlene's email with a lil encouragement.

> *... When I was at home this past time, while I was cleaning the attic, I found some letters that Mom had written to Pops when we were all in*

Mississippi without his trifling tail. Even then she was begging that nigga to step up and be a man. I think that's why I have had so many abortions, cause I am scared that I will be like him and my wife is going to have to beg me to handle my responsibilities. Mom said in her letter that Vick was just like him and as hateful as him. That nigga poisoned our older brother and he is trying to poison us with the same hate, but you gotta be strong and kill that hate with love, lil sister. I know it is easy for me to say and I am a thousand miles away, but I am pleading with you for your soul that you don't let that hate infect you cause that's what Satan wants. I love you. Stay strong and don't grow weary in well doing, for your season shall come soon.

Right now I will leave that topic alone cause I want to get to the scripture of the day cause I need a word from the Lord. Plus, I got to get some work done for my night class tonight although it's not a lot cause I managed my time this weekend well for the most part and got most of my work done. The scripture of the day is: *Take heed, brethren, lest there be in any of you an evil heart of unbelief, in departing from the living God. But exhort one another daily, while it is called Today; lest any of you be hardened through the deceitfulness of sin*

(Hebrews 3:12-13). This is a good scripture and the thing that sticks out in my mind is that the Bible constantly reminds us to stay watchful, diligent and always beware cause we as humans can be deceived by fleshly and worldly matters and this issue going on with the family is just one example of that.

We as the faithful Christian members of the family have to take heed and remember that it isn't our loved ones causing the hate and bitterness within us; it's Satan using them to stir up these feelings. We can cure them of Satan's hold though by loving them and trusting in God and not turning or departing from God and the ways He has showed us by cutting them off, judging and or ridiculing them—of which I am guilty because in my anger I couldn't hear Vick's plea to stop being so judgmental and listen to him. I couldn't listen because his foolish speech had already stirred the anger in me and caused God's Spirit to depart from me as soon as I heard him curse Mom, so these are things I have to watch lest it cause me to fall from grace.

The inspirational theme for the day is True to Ourselves. Today I will honor, cherish and love myself. When confused about what to do, I will be true to myself. I will break free of the hold others and their expectations have on me. I'm also going to pray that Deuce's girlfriend, Cardi's latest drama doesn't affect my mom or nephews.

29

ICEBERG SLIM'S PIMP

4:19 p.m. 11/9/04 The Morgan View Lab
I am what I am by the grace of God. Today has been a wonderful day so far. I meant to get back at you yesterday and drop a dime on how things were going but after class I ended up talking with Ms. Bethem then heading over to Herb's. At Herb's I ran into Jeff, the cat from the church that has a baby by the preacher's daughter. As soon as I saw him I told him I missed him. Loban was in the room so I didn't say at church. I just gave him a stare down when I said it to let him know I was sincere. I went over there to drop *King Arthur* back off to Herb cause he let me borrow it, but Loban had already taken it to him. It was missing from my room so I walked over there just to check and clear my head anyway.

After a couple of minutes over there reading my book, Jeff finally opened up to me and started telling me about Kandi, his baby momma, and why he can't be around her. I think I reached him yesterday cause I was able to relate and let him know that I am in deep as far as the world is concerned just like him. Before leaving, he let me know that he wanted to come to church but didn't want to have to ride with his baby momma. I really started feeling good then because throughout the conversation we had talked about God and some other issues that face real black men. Loban even got in on the conversation cause he knew some of the people we were talking about. Now I have the responsibility to go get this brother for church and bring him back to the Lord. It feels good to be able to do something for the Lord and I look forward to our meeting. I could look in his eyes and tell that he wasn't jiving or jacking, so I am going to do everything I can to help this young brother come back to the Lord. As far as his baby momma is concerned and how the church will look at him after he comes back will be a true test of the character of some of the members in the church. Will they accept him like the prodigal son or look down on him because they feel he ain't been taking care of his kid like he should be? We will see.

Okay, now back to something I mentioned earlier: my book. I am currently reading *PIMP* again by Iceberg Slim and I swear it is funny to me that although I ain't been to prison the cat Iceberg has similar thoughts, concerns and feelings as me. The crazy thing is that everything that has to do with pimping runs through Milwaukee and that is where this young cat gets his basic training—in the Mill and in Waupun and Green Bay's correctional facility. The things that he and Donald Goines's character Whoreson had to learn through mistakes are things that I picked up from somewhere without having to make the mistakes myself or get my heart broke. Another crazy thing is that I can't remember the last chick to break loose on me, and I've always had a stable in different area codes. The only major difference between me and these characters is that I've always had options and never had my back against the wall to where it was pimp or die.

As I read these stories and think about the real life stories that I have amassed in these few months, I know I would be rich by now had I put all of my pimping exploits down on paper when I was out there smoking and doing Mr.GoodGame in Waynesboro and on 5th in the Mill. I mean I feel like I've done it all except go out and strong arm by myself. Most of the cons that they mention in the books, I have done in one form or another at some point in my life. I even created my own hustles at a young age. Like when we was dead broke in Waynesboro, I would go to the dollar store and get some of our version of Cool Water cologne, take it out the box and sell it at school for 10, 15, sometimes 20 dollars. Fools would buy it cause I wore it and had chicks, and they just wanted to be like me. Crazy stuff, but it is going to be magnificent when God takes me where He wants me to be and people are able to see where I came from.

Today I had a meeting with the assistant dean of my school. He took me for a ride in his brand new Beemer[19] to Kinko's so we could get a poster size print out of the kiosk to be framed for the dean. We had a nice lil talk on the way down there. I told him about my aspirations to go to law school and he told me he would be more than happy to give me letters of recommendation or help me in any way he could. He also talked about how he and the dean were discussing my qualities and how they noticed I have a wonderful attitude and work good, even under extreme pressure. I told him my whole life is pressure and gave him a little bit of background about where I'm from. He knows people in high places and will be able to connect me, but the thing that stuck with me the most is the fact that he thought that I worked well under pressure. That really made me smile inside and appreciate all of the hell that I've been

---

[19] According to BMW's website, "The correct term for a BMW automobile is "bimmer" –"beemer" and "beamer" actually only refer to a BMW motorcycle. In this book, however, I was referring to the automobile.

through. Another thing that stuck with me from that experience was that he said he knows he is going to read about me someday, so I am going to make sure he does. Even though he "milk and cookies," he is an alright dude.

After we took care of the business at Kinko's, he brought me back to the school and brought me lunch so that is just one of the million ways that God has been blessing me. I haven't spoken with Dr. Freeman yet or his son, but I plan on doing so before this week is out to let him know my scores and my plans. It is getting around time to buckle down on these applications and just about everything is ready except that I have to pay $112 to be registered with LSDAS which is where the law schools get all of their information. Hopefully the Lord will bless me with those funds because I have fee waivers for a couple of schools.

After I got back, I went to the room and finished recording gospel songs on this tape I have. So now I got a gospel tape with Kirk and family, a capella C.O.C. music, R. Kelly and *Sister Act 2* music. It is the bomb! Anyway, I am going to try and leave early for church tonight so I can stop at Brother Dashings's to drop off his *Ray* DVD. No word from Charlene them yet, but I did get an email from Missy asking if I wanted to come out there cause she found a ticket for $112 so we will see. I can't give a scripture of the day cause the internet ain't working on this computer but hopefully I will be able to drop some jewels about what we discussed in class later tonight. God is good all the time and I pray nothing happens to the family over Cardi's situation with Deuce's mom. Peace and Blessings.

11:07 p.m. 11/9/04 The Morgan View Lab

God is good all of the time! He blessed me and had enough mercy on me to allow me to make it to men's study tonight with minimum gas. My gospel tape that I made is off the hook! I made it just in time for sweet hour of prayer. As I looked around, I noticed that my buddies Nancy and JuJu weren't there and they are usually there before me. They were late because something happened to JuJu and she wasn't going to come. I had a feeling that it was man trouble and she needed to talk to a guy. The thought just jumped in my head. It could have been Satan, but as soon as it happened I attributed it to the Spirit. I told her when I get my phone on to just hit me up if she ever needs to talk. Our class was wonderful and we discussed some of the qualities that act like antibodies in our walk for Christ against sin. We also talked about having a haughty spirit which is an issue that I have been dealing with for quite some time now.

Oh yeah! I emailed Missy back and let her know that I would come out there and chill with her if she bought a ticket. I just wouldn't be able to do it on Thanksgiving because Mom wanted me to come home, so we will see. Another thing that I am not sure if I mentioned or not, cause it really has been on the backburner, is that I have been doing some research on creating attraction in women because not only am I going to try to publish this but I am going to also try and publish a sort of Macking Guide cause the game is to be sold not told. All those who know me and might want to know the secret, I will be able to give them something.

Some of the things that I have picked up from my research that I already used but couldn't put into words I have been practicing on BlackPlanet so I don't have to worry about slipping. I can practice and still do what I have to do as far as my walk. Like I said though, this has been on the backburner for quite some time now and that's where it is going to stay until I change my mind.

Anyway, that research is pretty much done and I've accumulated enough information to the point where I can master some of the things that

I use that I didn't know I use. So I am working on becoming a master of my emotions and keeping ironclad feelings if that makes sense. Maybe these books ain't helping cause I am preparing my game to go out and be the biggest pimp from the Mill that the world has ever seen. Only thing is that I am not going to be a bad pimp. But when I get to where I'm going to be in life, people are going to know that young black boy from the Mill had some serious "G" about himself. The legacy is being written. My main task is to make sure that somehow someway the legacy will glorify Christ in the end and not me. So that is what I am working on at this point in time, having self-control and self-discipline to the point where I am so cold in this game that a woman will not be able to make me weak and slip and fall in my walk.

After church I went to Bro. Dashings's house to check up on him cause he wasn't at church and we ended up talking and watching the Mayorga versus Trinidad fight again on tape. While he was on the phone with his financial advisor, I read the various Bible books that he had on his couch. Boy, did I pick up some information. He had one book that had a bunch of sermons outlined and another book that told the history of the Old Testament in depth, so while he was talking I was soaking up information. Thank the Lord for Brother Dashings because he saw me reading and went and dug out another copy of the book with the sermons outlined and gave it to me. Now, metaphorically speaking, I have a case for the shells that I will be spitting out whenever my first sermon may be. I no longer have the excuse that I am not prepared because with the different topics and outlines, all I would need would be about an hour or day of preparation and I should be able to preach a sermon for at least 45 minutes through my knowledge of the word and my experiences. I just thank God for tonight because it is taking me a step closer to that goal. God is truly good!

30

TALK WITH GOD

11:05 a.m. 11/15/04 The School of Education Lab

God is good! I have no single reason for saying that. It is simply the truth and an affirmation that I am sure I am going to need this week in my fight against Satan. I am trying to have an attitude of gratitude, learning that I not only need to be content where I am at but thankful because God has spared me so many times that I didn't deserve it. Getting this week started off on the right foot, I want to start with the scripture of the day which is: *Humble yourselves therefore under the mighty hand of God, that he may exalt you in due time: Casting all your care upon him; for he careth for you* (1 Peter 5:6-7). I have cast my cares upon the Lord and I am going to leave them there. He knows my needs and my wants and He hasn't left me out in the cold yet, so I trust that He will do what He does and that is love me better than I love myself.

Last night I stood in front of the church and asked them to pray for me as I try to stay on the straight and narrow, and pray that I can lower myself and keep my ego out of the way so I can do God's will. I know the effectual fervent prayers of the righteous man availeth much so I am going to have help. I am just so thankful to God for His church, His word, love and the wisdom which He has bestowed upon me.

> *Heavenly Father, God of all God's, Most Powerful God I come to you at this time with a humble spirit and sincere heart of praise wanting to thank you for all of the many blessings you have bestowed upon me Lord. I thank you for your grace and mercy because I know that you have the power to end my life whenever you see fit and for this I say Thank You for another day which I know I didn't deserve. Lord, I come asking that you allow me to redeem the time and walk circumspectly making the most out of this brand new day which I have never seen before. Lord, I thank you for waking me up this morning in my right mind with an attitude to want to please and serve you.*

> *I ask that you allow the things which I have read, heard, learned and received about you and your word dwell richly in my heart and dominate my thoughts. Please protect my heart and my mind from devising wicked imaginations, lustful thoughts and sinful ideas. Lord, I*

ask that you put a hedge around my thoughts and allow the Spirit to provide a biblical verse for any sinful thoughts that Satan may try to cause to pop up in my head. Lord, I ask that you forgive me for any sins whether it be word, thought, or deed that I have committed against you and I ask that you help me to recognize and realize what those sins are and turn from them. Lord, I ask that you forgive me of those sins and hear my prayer.

Be with me as I go throughout this day and allow me to be a blessing to all those who I interact with, and allow me to do and be my best at whatever I put my hand and mind to. Lord, help me to allow my light to shine bright and I ask that you grant me the courage to open my mouth and speak on the things you would have me to speak on and to be silent when you would have me to be silent. Guide my steps and help me to acknowledge you in all I do. Lord, I pray that you help me to remember who I am and whose I am. Heavenly Father, I thank you for bringing me this far in life and I thank you for where I am at this exact moment. I also thank you for hearing my prayers and taking care of the family in my absence.

Thank you for the many blessings which you have bestowed upon them, Lord. I ask that you continue to watch over them and bless them. Be with Charlene, Lord and help her to continue to know the seriousness of the responsibility that she has to raise CJ right and help build his spiritual foundation. Lord, I ask that you help me to be the best role model and big brother that I can be. Be with Mom, bless her and strengthen her because she deserves it and you know she has been one of your hardest fighting soldiers for a long time. Heal her body if it be your will, Lord and bless her financially that she may be able to prosper and glorify you in her prosperity. Watch over the nephews and help them to realize that they won't make it far in life or where they wanna go without you. Help them to learn the principles of respect, education and discipline, Lord. Guide, protect and bless them as they go throughout life and help them to come to glorify you when it is all said and done, Father. Lord, be with Charity and Vick. Teach them to love and that family is all we got. Help them to love others as you love them.

Lord, just continue to watch over us all and bless us. I thank you for all of the hardships which we were allowed to go through and that we are going to go through. It is my prayer that you allow us to learn the lessons you would have us to learn from our trials and tribulations. These things I ask and give thanks for, in your wonderful son Jesus's name. AMEN.

Nuff said . . .

31

BACK IN THE ILL MILL

12:50 p.m. 11/26/04 In the Mill at Home
God is good! He allowed me to make it home to see the family safely and has been taking care of me ever since! The night I got here I chilled at home with the nephews until they went to sleep. Since it was my cousin Gloria's B-Day, I went out with her to BW3's. She looked out and got the wings and a Smirnoff for both of us and we just had fun kicking it and talking with each other.

Tuesday I was at the crib during the day, so I cleaned up. When the nephews got home, I made them do their homework and fed them. Charlene came home from work and we just kicked it and ribbed each other in the loving way that we do. Issa came over after she got off work cause I had called the night I got here. She's really growing into being an even more prettier woman than I thought. We caught up on old times and talked about future plans and got a deeper understanding about expectations from our relationship. I played it differently though since I know she can be full of ish, so I just was very "standoffish and nonchalant" about her and us. She told me this was how I was acting so I continued to carry it that way cause it was working. She kept dropping hints like "How long you expect me to wait for you?"

It was funny cause off top I was like "You like a lil sis to me," and since I got a fresh cut before I left, the waves were busting and I had a button-up on so she was looking like *this nigga is fine*. I could see it in her eyes. It sounds conceited, but I can only call it how I see it. Anyway, I was very evasive and was working on my online application as she talked. That kind of pissed her off and she threatened to leave, so I got up from the computer cause I didn't want to be rude. I sat on the couch beside her and it was a wrap! She begin getting in her feelings and dropping info left and right. Come to find out she living with a nigga. I played like I already knew and that seeing as how she was like my lil sis, that was nothing. When I said that, she started telling me that she liked the way I was acting although she didn't like it and yadi yadi ya.

Mom came home and we began setting up for her Tuesday night Bible study. I invited Issa down but she wasn't trying to go, so she just went down and hollered at Mom for a minute and then the magic statement came out her mouth! She said that I reminded her of Tip, her older brother! Translation: You the type of man that I can get with and I know you can handle me. It was a wrap so I let her finish talking to Mom, not paying her any attention, except trying to hurry up and get her out so we could start Bible study. I walked her outside and she began telling me how she felt about us and the way I made her feel in the short time she was over here. She also told me that although she was with ol boy, she had confidence that I knew how to get her if I really wanted her. With that said, I am going to let her be until I am ready. She's cool right where she at. Let another nigga mold her. I'm just trying to show her how a roller can roll her. She was supposed to come over the next day but never came. Same ol Issa. I still got a soft spot in my heart for her cause she was my first crush, but I got a feeling it would get out of hand if we go deeper cause I know how to work her and vice versa.

The next day I went to school with Charity for Grandparents and Special Friends Day, so I had to get up at 6 and drop Charlene off at work for the car. Charity really enjoyed me being there (although she didn't say it) and I could tell she was proud of me cause she introduced me to everybody. She's a pretty popular girl at school and her lil friends were all up in my grill slobbering. I could tell Charity wanted to show me off cause I told her

I wasn't going unless she ironed my clothes the night before and she actually did it. She didn't use no spray starch but she ironed them nonetheless. We picked up her friend from home and ran into another one of her friends at the school, who's a straight up goof. I kind of embarrassed the teacher cause she gave them their vocabulary words and an activity, and I outdid the teacher. Since she was sitting beside me, she cut it short. She asked everybody to make one long sentence and see how many words they could use in that sentence. She had 9 and I had 18. Charity saw the reaction though and was proud of her older brother.

They only had a half a day so when school was over we picked up Fat Mack and Billy and went to Pizza Hut. I fed the kids and watched *The Wire* while they played with each other and got on my nerves. Charlene came back and took Charity to work without following my command to put up the food that Mom had brought home to cook for Auntie Mavel's Thanksgiving event. When Mom came home she snapped and was in her feelings and just gave us a verbal beating. We listened and tried to feel her then did our part and tried to help and stay under her radar by slicing vegetables and doing what she asked. Mom was up cooking like she does late into the night. When I woke up the next morning, of course by my loving nephew CJ and his overgrown Trouty momma, Mom was already at the building with Aunt Mavel. This time Charlene had the instructions. The night before I told that heffa what Mom wanted and she told me to do it and dipped. So when Mom started going off, I tried to cover for her, but Mom jumped on me so I told her the truth.

Vick was also here cooking and it was good to see the family together; Vick even said it. I did my part and did the downstairs kitchen. I think we made Mom happy cause when she got back things were taken care of and she had clean dishes and space to do whatever she needed. We ended up loading the cars and going to the building and helping Aunt Mavel setup. All in all it was a huge success, no drama and it was all love. We got a couple of domino games going, some Tonk for quarters, and lots of socializing. I took my camera, so I got everybody and the food on tape. There was more than enough food and everybody brought a dish. After it was over, Charlene and I dipped. Vick didn't come, but that's cause he stuck playing San Andreas.

When I woke up, Mom had another talk with us and explained what we had done right and wrong the past couple of days and what we needed to work on. She really wants us to stick together as a family and love each other and carry on her giving tradition. Charlene broke her heart and told her in so many words that she wasn't trying to carry it on. We dealt with that and with my pimpish ways and Charity's introvert behavior and low self-esteem. After we had our family pow wow, we put all the food up, organized the refrigerator and cleaned Mom's kitchen.

Afterwards, I hit the streets and went and hollered at Vick. Him and OG Bobby Johnson was playing San Andreas and showing me the game. Right away I knew where I would be able to find Vick for the remainder of my stay here cause that game is gangsta and addictive as hell. Keeping it real though, I dipped and went and hollered at Lil Landry cause I said I was and we ended up going to this new club called 414. It was on and cracking, plenty of jump downs or JDs[20] which made me realize there is no place like home. Since I don't do the things I used to though, it kind of seemed strange being in there. I really didn't feel like stepping to no chicks cause I didn't have a place to take them and I ain't where I want to be at this point as

---

20 Urban Dictionary describes a "jump down" or "JD" as a person, usually female, who has sexual relations, especially oral, with many people for little or no gain.

far as materialistic things. Call it low self-esteem or whatever, but I basically breezed through like a pimp not thirsting over nothing cause one day, Lord's will, they ain't gone be able to see me and that's how I carried it. I was chosen several times with the eyes, but I played it cool and just chilled in the cut. After we left, we ended up watching the game until like 6 in the morning.

One important thing, at least to me, has been left out. I ain't got no butt and ain't really chilled with a female except Issa. Now that's scary and I sho hate to say it, but I really would like to dig off in something before I leave. All of the numbers I be using is dead though except Jasmine and I ain't trying to sweat her so I'm just short! Today I am probably going to just go get on the game wit Vick them and stay out of trouble.

32
BILLY'S BAPTISM AND BIG NEWS

4:11 p.m. 11/29/04 The Crib in the Mill
This morning I woke up cause of the grace and mercy of God, and because my ace, Kevin called finally. I was so sleepy though that I couldn't rap with him but for a second. Yesterday was a very eventful day. I got in early Sunday morning at about 2:00 cause I was playing that doggone San Andreas. That is one very addictive game. Anyway, I fought Satan off and got ready for church Sunday morning cause the buzz was that Billy was going to get baptized. Cardi and Ciara even came to church with us. Charity stayed at home cause she went and got some braids put in her head for her trip to Florida that her school is paying for.

Well Billy did get baptized and he asked me to go down front and hold his hand so I did. Ciara went up front with Mom, and Mom was crying cause she was so happy for Billy. I shed a few tears of joy too. I made sure to let him know I was proud of him. After church, we went out to eat when Cardi said she would have went down front but she didn't want to mess up her tracks. Billy told her that God could give her some real hair. That moment was so funny, but it hit Cardi so hard that she couldn't say anything. I think he is going to have some type of positive influence on her. After we left, I went home and took a nap until evening service.

At evening service, we did a welcome service for Billy then I was hit with some big news! When I get back, Brother Gains is going to have me preach a Sunday evening sermon, so it is time to step up. I spoke with Sheila and she said she is going to come down wit some of her folks to hear me preach. The time that I spend in Baltimore is going to be studying and preparing my sermon. I spent all night playing San Andreas until 6 in the morning. That's a doggone shame! I gotta pray for Vick. This morning I got up and cleaned up the upstairs and downstairs and washed clothes since I slept for most of the day. Tomorrow I am supposed to go and see Brother and Sister Loving, so I am looking forward to that.

33

TEACHING OTHERS HOW TO PRAY

5:32 p.m. 12/9/04 The Morgan View Lab
God is good. I can't even front. Yesterday's class with the boys was a smash! I think I enjoyed it just as much as they did. We talked about self-esteem and self-image issues. The boys were very receptive and eager to learn what I had to teach them. It was so real that a couple of the times, instead of me having to quiet the room down and regain their attention, some of the students' peers was like "Ay, look yo. I'm trying to learn, so let him teach." It really was fun and I can't wait til next Wednesday. I can see from here on out as long as I don't do anything to lose the respect I have, I am going to have no problems teaching this class. I was prepared and had in my mind how much time I wanted to designate to each discussion and activity because I overlooked my lesson and lesson plan before I went to class.

I pulled the boys' coats about being leaders, why some of them dress the way they dress for the most part, and how to gain influence and brush hate off at the same time. They were curious to know why I was dressed up and when I explained to them about the conversation I had had with Brother Dashing about how I felt about having to dress up, yet I still did it, I could tell they gained even more respect for me. I told them I had to sacrifice my beliefs and humble myself and learn how to dress like a man if I was going to teach them how to be men effectively. A man sometimes has to humble himself, so they learned that important lesson too!

At the end of the class I asked for a volunteer to pray and close us out. The preacher's son volunteered. I asked him before he prayed if he was going to pray for real cause I didn't want him to do no rudy pooh rushed through prayer when someone in the room may have wanted to take that opportunity and use it to grow and get closer to God. He said he was going to be for real so I let him close us out. He mumbled a rushed through prayer like it was his first time talking to God and he was scared of God or at least didn't know who he was, so I lectured him about that and explained to the boys when you pray you talk to God as if you know Him because He is supposed to be your best friend and your father. I gave another young brother a chance and he did a rushed through prayer too, so I broke it down to them in street terms.

It went something like this (I am proud of my analogy because the boys understood it and

I know they gone give me their best effort next week). I told them they are supposed to talk to God on the regular like they talk to their earthly best friend. "Talk to Him as if you know Him," I said. "A prayer could contain prayers of thanksgiving, supplication and intercession." They knew what prayers of thanksgiving were but they really couldn't put into words prayers of thanksgiving in the spiritual sense. I used the analogy that we all are getting beat up daily by a bully, which is Satan. God is our best friend and we need to ask Him for help. If He was our earthly friend, before we asked for His help, we would talk to Him and thank Him for all the times He had our back—especially for that time He had our back in 3rd grade when the bully had us cornered and the times in the 6th, 7th and 8th grade.

They seemed to understand the analogy well. "Next," I said, "you would ask your friend to help you prepare for the next fight. So you would ask for a Mack 10, 2 nines, 3 45's and a shotgun cause yo enemy is packing some heat." The boys really liked this analogy and got the understanding of what prayers of supplication meant: supplies.

They asked what prayers of intercession were and I told them, "After you talked to your best friend and he said he had your back and gave you what you needed, you would realize that you only have two trigger fingers, so you could only shoot two guns at once. Therefore you would need him to come and intercede or interrupt on your part. In other words, you would give him a time and a place to come through." They basically took it as a meeting ground where God would meet us and help us.

They came up with examples like in the hall when that girl slapped me or hit me and I'm ready to "bang her" (as they say). Anyway after the analogy, the pastor's son asked me for a second chance and I gave it to him. In the middle of the prayer, the door opened and he hurried up and ended because it threw his thought pattern off. I told him don't let nothing stop you from praying to your God. Then I explained how he would have to pray sometimes later in life, through all kinds of symbolic storms and turmoil. He agreed and said next time he will continue, so I finally let them go but we were like 15 minutes late. Anyway, class was a success and I just thank God that He used me to teach the boys some valuable lessons. Brother Dashings came and got me for class and treated me to chicken afterwards.

This morning I got up on time. School was cool and everything went over all smooth, with no problems. Thing is though, every time I dress up I think it is really a distraction to the students, especially the girls but even some of the dudes too. Crazy. I'm thinking about doing my research paper on that, but I am not sure how I would go about it.

1:10 p.m. 12/10/04 The School of Education Lab

Last night I spoke with Missy and Nancy for a good lil while before taking a late night nap. Afterwards, I got up, got fresh dressed, and went over to Herb's and got on the game til about 3 in the morning, whooping niggas in Live and Knockout Kings. I still was a Christian surrounded by hell though—smoke and what most would consider thugs. I still have my influence over there. I can tell cause a new dude was there and out of my peripheral I could see him examining me. When I turned down the blunt, he really begin to wonder who I was, although I shook up wit everybody including him when I came in. I'm sure he noticed that I took care to choose my words wisely and not cuss, but he was stuck on the fact that I was the flyest cat in the room with the pimp juice, but I wasn't trying to fit in. I know he was definitely wondering what I was doing there and where

I was from seeing as how I wasn't partaking in the "festivities." He eventually just came out the mouth and asked me.

Cause of my creases, he asked if I was from down south. When I said no but I spent some time down there he said he knew it cause of the killer crease in my jeans. There was no hate in his voice, yet admiration. When I told him I went to Jackson State, he told me he spent 4 years of high school in Jackson and we cliqued from that point on. We were talking bout how much love it is in the south and how it's way more popping than Baltimore. I ended up sticking over there longer than I expected cause me and this nigga was boxing on the game and he was actually competition, winning 2 out of 4 games. That's more than I'm used to losing cause everybody else is usually so high and drunk that they can't focus.

I got up this morning and got dressed and was surprised to reach the lab and get a call from Vick. He was telling me how he's been talking to Bobby about saving his soul and getting right with God. From what I was getting from the conversation, he sounded serious and me crying over his soul in our last real conversation affected him. Sounds like God is doing some feeding and watering, and I am ever so thankful. The Lord is great and He knows that was just the motivation I needed to get on the grind and tighten up my sermon cause I ain't been looking at it like I should. I've been satisfying my earthly lust but hopefully that will change tonight.

The scripture of the day is: *And they overcame him by the blood of the Lamb, and by the word of their testimony; and they loved not their lives unto the death* (Revelation 12:11). That's good! I love my life too much, matter of fact I have always loved my life and that's why it has taken me so long to get to this point. Well that is something that I am going to have to get over cause I got to remember that I am just passing through here. It is not my life to love.

9:05 p.m. 12/12/04 The Morgan View Lab
I know I'm slipping cause each time I sit down to the computer I feel overwhelmed with how much I need and want to say as far as what is going on in my life. So in one big breath, I am exhaling, and here we go . . . God is good! That's first and foremost. Friday, I helped the church setup for the men's prayer breakfast. That was cool because it felt good to be in the house of the Lord although I was the only brother under 30 there as usual. It was only about six of us but we got the tables and

chairs setup and I enjoyed the fellowship with my Christian brothers and sisters. I also got some advice from Brother Clint and Brother Fason, who are both preachers, about preparing to preach.

Afterwards I called Paul cause I wanted to hang out with someone from the church but he didn't answer so I left him a message hoping he would call me before I got too far away from the area, but I received no call which led to a serious mental and spiritual battle. I called Brother Dashings and he answered and said I could come over and help him with his presentation that he had to give Saturday morning at the men's prayer breakfast. I went over there and got some valuable advice and tips from him about ministering and allowing God to use me as a minister. He basically told me to slow my roll and let God use me the way he wants to use me and don't stress about my sermon by making it an event, cause then it becomes about me. We ended up burning the midnight oil. In helping him, I got some valuable scriptures and divine inspiration just by searching and studying the scriptures with him.

His topic that he was given was to talk about where you will be when Jesus returns. In talking and preparing his topic, I ended up deciding that I wasn't going to take the easy way out and preach a feel good sermon. The Spirit led me to believe that I needed to preach what needed to be preached and not worry about certain members in the audience pointing out my flaws and sins. Satan had really been working on me concerning things coming back to slap me in the face and me bringing reproach on the church.

Well sitting and talking with Brother Dashings and studying the scriptures with him pointed me toward my new sermon which will be "The Longsuffering of God." That is a topic which I could speak on without an outline for hours on hand cause God is truly that good and has and still is longsuffering with me. Just being there and burning the midnight oil gave me the confidence and the Spirit to know God is qualifying me. It doesn't matter what I did in the past cause of what God did with Paul. I am approved by God and that is all that counts; my audience really doesn't matter. I was called for a purpose and that is to proclaim the gospel, not sugarcoat the Word and give the people what they want to hear so they will like me. Who am I trying to persuade, men or God? Nuff said.

After I left there I went home and got in the bed cause I had to get up early in the morning for the men's prayer breakfast. Saturday morning I got up on time by the grace of God. When I called Brother Dashings to see if he was woke, cause he was supposed to be coming to get me, he had just got up so I ended up having to drive up to the church. When I got there, it was wonderful cause we had even more brothers than we had last time and we had some good speakers and there was some powerful things to be learned. There were five different speakers, so I observed five different styles and it helped me observe which one was more fit to me and that is the style of shooting from the hip and talking what I know, not really worrying about an outline. So I am going to have three major points in my sermon.

After I left there, I went home and prepared for my Bible study which I was going to have with Freeway at 1:30, but she didn't answer the phone. She called me at about 3 saying she wasn't going to be able to make it cause she had stuff to do. Well I got in the bed and took a nap and was actually kind of down cause I had been looking forward to teaching her since Tuesday night when Brother Bethem gave the men's class the "90 Minutes and In" program. It's designed to teach people Biblical fundamentals and show them the importance of baptism. After I took my nap, Freeway called again and said that she wanted me to call her after the play so I told her I would cause she still wanted to study. I got up out of bed and got dressed for the play cause Nancy called and said she was on her way.

We went to see Langston Hughes's *Black Nativity*. Funny thing was that neither of us had tickets and we were going to buy them at the door, but they were sold out. So we just sort of hung around til we got tickets cause we knew we were highly favored. Boy, were we right! We ended up having some of the best seats in the house, 3rd row on the side where all the action was at and where one of the members of the cast who happened to be the funniest was stationed. Most of the play was a depiction of a Baptist church and on our side was the fresh old man who did all the dances when he caught the Spirit and fell asleep snoring during church; it was quite funny. After the play Nancy came back to the crib with me and I heated up some of the leftovers from the men's prayer breakfast and we got our grub on. She had gotten comfortable and taken her shoes off and I could tell she was trying to chill, but I was trying to get rid of her cause I had told P and Herb I would go to this Jamaican party with them.

Before I could put Nancy out, I got a call from Freeway saying she was in Morgan View and was willing to do the study and wanted to come up. So I was going to put Nancy out, then the Spirit told me to ask her to stay. It was something I saw on her face that let me know she really wasn't trying to leave cause she looked real comfortable. She jumped on the opportunity and I was kind of mad at first cause I knew that's what she wanted from the start, but I let it go.

Freeway came in and I introduced her and we chitchatted for like three minutes. While they talked, I went and got the Bibles and some paper. To make a long story short, the Lord got His shine on and I went through the study effortlessly. He gave me some wonderful examples and analogies. Afterward I asked if she wanted to be saved and told her the story about Philip and the Eunuch and she said yeah. I started calling the brothers trying to get the church open. Eventually I got ahold of Brother Bethem and he said he would beat us there.

God is good! So we drove up there and she got baptized and we drove her home. This morning she was up and ready to go to church cause Nancy played bus driver and got me, JuJu and Freeway. Now that the Lord used me to help bring Freeway to the fold on my first try with the "90 Minutes and In" format, knowing that I hid a multitude of my sins, had me confident that I can do it again. I now have a spiritual swagger and feel like I can bring the truth to anyone with an honest heart.

Brother Bethem and I were talking early Sunday morning at the church. He said, "Good job, Charlie. Just 2000 more to go." The crazy thing is that I knew he was joking, but I felt like it was a very attainable goal. Not only is it attainable but the other crazy thing is that the first soul that popped up in my heart, that I am sure now the Lord could use me to save, is Lala. How crazy is that? I spoke with Sheila about it because it is something that I want to do and I know I owe it to God, Lala and myself. I tried to teach Lala before but to no avail probably because of my behavior and some of the things we went through. With her, I actually believe I brought shame and reproach upon the church. I hope God will use me to make things right. I told her once that I love her and because I love her, I cared about her soul. And I still do, so now that I have the knowledge and wisdom to guide her to the truth, I feel it is my responsibility. I communicated all this to Sheila and told her to pray about the situation because I am unsure of God's plan and I would be praying too. I want her to pray because I have a swagger from Jesus now and I am confident that she will see the truth and be able to turn from her ways. How do we interact or where do we go once she is saved? I just want to do right by God, Sheila and Lala.

Once Lala is saved I may feel a sense of responsibility to help her grow in Christ and she may want me to be her man. What she wants is not important but once I save her I don't want her to turn from the truth because of me like she did the first time I tried to teach her. So that is the current issue, but I ain't sweating it major like that cause I have faith that God will make things alright. They came and got me for church cause Freeway spent the afternoon with Nancy them cause she cooked dinner. When they picked me up, they had a plate for me and that was cool, but I had to wait til after church to eat it. I was proud that Freeway came back to church in the evening cause most new converts don't do that. Heck, most older members don't do that and Brother Bethem noticed and noted it during his sermon.

34

MOCHA RETURNS . . .

10:17 a.m. 12/13/04 City College Laptop
I am in class right now and things are pretty calm because students are busy working on their projects. A lot of the students are asking me why I am here and I want to say because I love the kids, but I can't let them know that so I've been telling them it's because I got work to do.

Last night after leaving the lab, I spoke with Sheila on the phone and she was really discouraging but truthful. She told me she thought my whole motivation behind telling her that I wanted to save Lala's soul was selfish. She also feels I should slow down on this preaching bit, that when she first met me she felt my motivation for wanting to do it was as if it was all about me. That's what stuck with me most. I learned that in my language I am still talking as if it is all about me. I sensed the same thing from Brother Dashings, as if my words were being twisted around. It's just the confidence in which I speak and the faith that I have that God can use me. I have been getting hit from all sides and it is kind of discouraging, but I ain't gone let anybody be the judge of whether or not I can serve God. After speaking with her, I felt kind of angry but I look at it as a good thing because it seems as if I am being prepared.

It has been a real humbling experience. After last night, I kind of decided that I am going to do this once and leave it alone because people are already judging me based on my past. Even my own mother joked with Charlene and said I was going to bring damnation upon the family, so I am going to be easy and slow my roll like everybody is telling me. The more I analyzed the conversation with Sheila, the more I believed that her feelings of my motivation was actually a reflection of how she felt about the situation and the advice that she gave me. Because I respect her and I did ask for her opinion, I am not going to try and reach Lala for a Bible study. Heck, Charlene even said she don't think I am strong enough to try and do that yet.

Anyway, today has started off pretty good and I am going to close this out for now.

8:51 a.m. 12/15/04 City College Laptop
Today started real early, but God is still good. At like three in the morning I heard the fire alarm going off in my building, and it went off for like two hours after I first heard it. I tried to go back to sleep but that didn't work. Last night I went to the church and helped to clean it up because Brother

Dashings drove me, and he and I are in the same care group. We had a good time talking about different issues, but I missed sweet hour of prayer. During men's studies, Brother Bethem came in and spoke to us again about the program "90 Minutes and In."

On the way home I had a talk with Brother Dashings about some of the politics in church and it came out that we have no elders or deacons because men don't want to step up and be held accountable or be responsible. I found out a whole lot about the church last night and I was kind of disappointed, but we prayed before I got out the car and those thoughts eventually vanished. I was pissed before I got out the car though cause in so many words Brother Dashings told me that the same men that be acting like they giving it all up for God don't want to give their lives up. I went to thinking about exactly what I gave up, got pissed and felt like crying.

Mocha called me two nights ago. We used to work together and would hookup often after work. She told me she didn't answer the last time I called her because she was in the N.O. She also shared that she married the 38 year old chump who didn't know he had a straight out freak. She told me she's back working at channel 17, where we worked together, and wants to get with me because her husband still ain't satisfying her. He actually told her she's boring in bed. Now that was funny cause this girl is down for whatever whenever. Back when we were coworkers, she would come to 5th street after work and we'd freak til the early morn (and she loves dancing). Not only would she come over to 5th but she'd clear the coast for me to go over to her crib and wear it out too. She is just a sexy individual, a thick brick house. Not the prettiest thing but sexy nonetheless because she is very experienced and likes to wear teddies and lingerie and meet her man at the door with nothing but stilettos on and she can really get down.

Anyway, I am going to really have to pray and do some soul-searching cause I went back to thinking about some things I shouldn't have last night. I also drilled Missy about how I could take her places but she had to pass certain tests and do what I tell her. In other words Mr.GoodGame is really trying to come back. I'm fighting it with all my heart but I'm getting from all fronts that I probably should do this once and leave it alone for a while. I really want to step up and do what God would have me to do. So yo boy is really going to need some prayer.

10:24 p.m. 12/16/04 Home in the Mill
I just arrived home about 45 minutes ago and I went through it on the plane ride here. Before I get into that though, let me play catchup real fast because I feel like I am going to be at this computer all night. Last night after church, JuJu and Nancy showed up at my door to scoop me for dinner. We dropped JuJu off at home to clean her house and get started on the food, and Nancy and I headed to her house to get more food and seasoning. Her goofiness or should I say corny joy wore off on me and we had a good ride over there. When we reached JuJu's it was like we had arrived at a hotel. Her apartment was nice and big; she even had a deck attached to her room. I ended up being over there til like 2:30 in the morning. They didn't finish the food til like 1:30 but I was cool cause I was watching the Suns destroy the Jazz on JuJu's TV which looked like a 52 inch. She has DirectTV so I told them in order for me to go to dinner with them we had to go to her house. I am not sure Nancy liked this, but I really wasn't trying to go cause I had ate McDonald's for lunch and wasn't all that hungry. Anyway we ate and had a merry old time.

This morning when I got up for school, I really wanted to just turn back over and play dead, but I got up and did what I had to do. Everything was cool but after lunch I decided that I wasn't going back to school cause I wanted to sleep so that is what I did. I slept and played a game of Live for my dynasty mode. Well Nancy came and got me to take me to the airport, but it seemed like it took her forever to get to me. When she finally did make it, it seemed like I was riding with Mom. I just tried my best to stay positive and keep my mouth shut cause I was thoroughly irked by her. I think it was because she told me that she would be over at my house to get me in 15 minutes and it ended up taking her 30 minutes to get there, so I had plenty of time to think to myself. During the ride she was trying to talk to me, not catching the hint that I just wanted to get to the airport on time and make it back to Milwaukee as soon as I could. It seemed like she was driving to get on my nerves, just cruising along. She got in every line at every light and missed what seem like every light that she could possibly miss to talk to me. I just put my face in my coat to hide my aggravation cause I knew I was pissed at her for no reason. I was just going through one of my satanic mood swings.

I made it just in time to catch my flight. On the flight, I had a battle and a talk with God. I actually had tears in my eyes cause I know that thinking about Mocha is wrong and I was trying my hardest to keep those thoughts out but my mind kept trying to make me plan how I would see her. I prayed, sang and even tried staring out the window trying to meditate and go to another place in my mind, but I couldn't shake the thought of penetrating her. In my mind and heart, I felt like I might as well have already hit it cause my thoughts were that sinful. I was thinking about calling Brother Gains and asking to preach the Sunday after next so I could hit it and have a chance to get back right with God, even though I know that is dead wrong. I started tearing up cause even that thought to me is sinful enough to be struck down and not wake up another day. I felt horrible and Satan was trying to get me to just give up, but I ain't—even though I know I am chief of sinners. That is so true of me. I am in heat and horny as hell . . . literally.

Mocha, in my mind, is looking real good and I actually thought about putting God off for another week. I even thought about just totally turning my back on God and ignoring him for all five minutes of a chance to be with a chick who I always knew was just as sinful as me. I told her to call me when she got off work and it is nearing that time. I don't want to go that route, so before I got off the plane I made up my mind to call Brother Gains when I got home to let him know I am in town. I wanted some inspiration and also to setup a time to talk with him in person. Satan knows where I am weak and he brought just the type of girl who I would jump through loops on the low to have a freaky night with. I am struggling terribly.

Afterwards I felt like a punk because it is a simple choice, choose God or choose Satan. If I choose those five minutes of lust, my heart will probably be heavy for the rest of my life knowing I got in the pulpit all wrong. I know that's all it's going to take cause she has an excellent technique because she is a dancer and I ain't had none in a while. So I am really struggling and I have no idea how I am going to handle the situation. Mom is here trying to counsel me since she heard me on the phone with Brother Gains. She wants me to start feeling my feelings and so here goes:

Right now I feel scared because I really want to go and break Mocha off tonight if she calls. I know it's dead wrong and I fear the consequences from God. I really want to feel the Spirit come down upon me and take these thoughts out of my head and give me the joyful feeling of thankfulness that I keep trying to meditate on. I know that God doesn't give us a spirit of fear, so I know that even feeling scared is wrong. It's almost as if I want to cry out to God and beg for mercy in advance or ask Him to take this cup from me. That thought leads me back to my conversation with God when the Spirit told me that what I am going through is nothing compared to what Christ had to go through. All I got to do is make a simple choice to do right, but He had to deal with dying for something that He didn't do. While on the plane, all of a sudden "Man up" repeated in my heart over and over, and that helped for a minute.

I hate that I am not married, because Satan knows I am still weak in this area and can be taken in this area because of my lustful desires. I can do all things through Christ who strengthens me. God has blessed me with knowledge to know what is right and wrong and exactly what His word says. He has equipped me, so for me to fall means I am too lazy to stand. He has blessed me with the ability to stand tall, yet I want to slump down and act as if I don't know how to stand. The person or thing that can really push my buttons is a sexy female and the thought of sex when I ain't had none in so long.

I can change how I view women by respecting them and not just seeing them as a means to justify my ends. I can control how I look at them when I see them on a daily basis if I just focus and concentrate hard enough on not sinning through the lust of the flesh. I am grateful for all of the blessings that God has bestowed upon me and I feel horrible just thinking about sinning against God after all that He has brought me through. He's kept me safe from AIDS, death in the club or streets, He's fed me, clothed me and blessed me with wisdom and knowledge. I am really sad still because deep in my heart I want to just say forget it and go have my night of sexual pleasure, but I am going to resist the devil, at least tonight.

I feel like the rich man who came up to Jesus and asked what he must do to be saved. Jesus said sell all your possessions and come and follow me. The rich man was saddened and turned and left because he had many things and didn't want to sell them. I had a glorious life and am still trying to hold on to it. That is the problem: I haven't submitted all the way. Pray for me. Lord, have mercy on my soul . . .

*

At this point in my journey, I was successful in my battle with my smoking addiction but failing miserably in overcoming my sex addiction. My newfound self-awareness allowed me to be honest and admit to my failures in the sexual realm. An old African Proverb states that success in life largely depends on how you handle your failures. True failure is not falling but the refusal to get up. Since I acknowledged my failures, it helped me to get back up when I fell. Each time I fell was an opportunity to learn more about myself and my triggers. In addition, I moved closer to walking in my purpose because each time I fell, I gained invaluable experience on how to overcome a similar obstacle in the future. Sometimes your purpose can be found in your failures and the pain you experience as a result.

This part of the journey included different triggers and obstacles, including some unforced errors on my part that kept me from being sober—physically, mentally and spiritually. From these experiences, I was again reminded of (or learned) several lessons which now help me to walk in my purpose. I highlight these lessons hoping they will help you in your walk:

1. Always keep it real with yourself.
Because it's possible to deceive yourself. While I was no longer struggling to get sober in the physical sense as far as smoking is concerned, I wasn't sober sexually, so I was failing. I was intoxicated with my ego and still struggling. When trying to minister to others, I've learned that it helps people to relate to you more when you are honest

about your shortcomings. Admitting to failure is scary because it makes us feel vulnerable, but it's surprising just how anxious being vulnerable can make us. We want people to think we are all that and a bag of chips! Admitting to failures doesn't fit into our agenda. Plus, not knowing how people will react is scary.

However, I've learned that being my most authentic self requires me to be vulnerable and share my failures as well as my successes because those experiences help make me who I am. I call it "taking the mask off." When I meet people now, even in a professional setting, I'm no longer wearing a mask and it is so liberating! I'm *Black AF*[21] and I don't spend much mental energy trying to conform to my environment anymore. Interestingly, I've found that many times the environment will conform or gravitate to me. Those I engage with also feel liberated because they quickly recognize that they can speak freely and take their mask off as well. You want a secret to building deep relationships? Practice being vulnerable and watch what happens.

---

21 *Black AF* is a popular Netflix American sitcom created by and starring Kenya Barris (creator of Blackish). It provides a fictionalized glimpse into Kenya's life at home with his six kids. #**blackAF** uncovers the messy, unfiltered and often hilarious world of what it means to be a "new money" **black** family trying to "get it right" in a modern world where "right" is no longer a fixed concept. Black AF stands for Black As F^@%.

2. Keep the main thing the main thing.

Some of my failures and situations I found myself in were unforced errors. However, I realized that I could stress over these failures and wallow in self-pity or I could let go and let God. Sometimes that's easier said than done, but as you've read, I had to redirect my thoughts. As my co-lead of our young adult ministry always stresses to our students, "We got to keep the main thing the main thing." The main thing for me was to trust that God would see me through whatever mess I found myself in—even if it was self-inflicted. Things will not always be easy when you are trying to do right and find your purpose. Even Jesus told his apostles to expect to be persecuted! From a very young age, my mom instilled in me the lesson of Proverbs 3:5-6. It basically says trust in the Lord with all your heart and lean not unto your own understanding, acknowledge Him in all your ways and He will direct your path. The lesson? Keep the main thing the main thing and that's to trust in God.

3. There is no progress without struggle.

That struggle may come in the form of a sacrifice. It took a long time but one lesson I learned has to do with the understanding of Matthew 16:25. This was a particularly difficult scripture to understand early in my life. Now I always share with students in my young adult ministry that the Bible is relevant at all times and Matthew 16:25 is so true. It states: *For whosoever will save his life shall lose it: and whosoever will lose his life for my sake shall find it.*

Along your journey, similar to mine, it often will feel like you are missing out on things in the world when you are trying to walk in purpose for God. Why? Walking in purpose for God requires you to be sanctified or set apart. It's what makes you unique and gives you your "vibe." When you are set apart, life is different, and as you've learned, you need to change your environment, people and thoughts. FOMO (fear of missing out) is real. However, I've learned through experience that as a Christian, "friendship with the world" can come at a great cost to your joy, peace, mental and physical health, and bank account. I use the example of how stupid I felt when I was younger after I would go out to the club on Friday nights and end up getting my kicks dirty after spending a bunch of money, which I quite frankly didn't have, for outfits, transportation, admission, food and drinks. I've lost my cell phone and wallet while going out several times. Add to that the guilt and worry after one-night stands and you may understand the insanity of looking forward to going out the following Friday and doing it all over again based on a fear I may miss out on some fun.

That is exactly what I used to do and what I know many look forward to doing, despite the cost. Sacrificing your life for Christ's sake, I've learned, and not doing those things will actually add to your joy, peace, mental and physical health, and your bank account.

4. Understand that sometimes you are the problem in a relationship or situation.

We all are capable of being toxic. Reflecting on how I treated women and how I was so quick to dismiss their concerns makes me realize I was very toxic. Most of my actions and patterns of behaviors were unjustifiable. In the relationship with Nia, I was nothing more than a taker. To be fair, I warned her when I first met her in no uncertain terms that curiosity killed the cat but she pursued and didn't listen. Everything happens for a reason and we both learned a couple of lessons about relationships from that experience—namely, when people show you who they are, believe them. My mom always says you can tell a tree by the fruit it bears. Seek to master the art of listening and observing.

Lala taught me you will learn a lot by doing so. Related, one of my "mask off" understandings that I often share in applicable situations is that "Niggas gone nigg if you let them." With Nia, I was allowed to "nigg" or just take what I want and so I "nigged." People will treat you how you allow them to treat you and behave in a manner that is tolerated in a particular environment.

5. Don't expect you from others.

Don't expect people to behave, think or talk like you because we are all unique individuals with unique experiences. Interestingly, today's "cancel culture" may deprive us of valuable opportunities to sharpen our emotional intelligence by learning to deal with difficult individuals. For example, I deal with a bunch of folks that I don't particularly like (and think are toxic), but it may be necessary to deal with them for a short period of time in order to accomplish a particular objective. However, make sure you aren't in a position where you have to depend on a person who you believe is not solid or dependable. If you manage relationships according to these principles, it will likely save you a lot of frustration and disappointment and help you appreciate people as flawed humans trying to find their way just like you.

6. Accept that sometimes the difficult individuals that trigger you can be family members.

At this part of the journey, I really struggled with harshly judging my pops and brother for their perceived failures. I had lost respect for both and blamed them for some of the hardships in my life due to their failure to "step up and be men." However, I've learned to accept people as they are because life is too short to hold grudges. I once heard a preacher say that holding a grudge is like drinking poison and expecting the other person to die. Life has taught me that grudges are not worth holding; we should seek to extend the same grace and mercy to others that we ask God to give to us. To illustrate this lesson, let me fill you in on how my relationships with my pops and Vick ended.

My pops died in 2019. The family decided to move him from Milwaukee down to Atlanta near the end of 2017 because he wasn't able to take care of himself and properly administer the medicines he needed to survive. Charity and I were opposed to the move for various reasons (mainly resentment), but eventually Mom's Christian plea caused me to relent and I was the deciding vote. I was opposed because I knew it would cost me and my family financially and because I had not yet forgiven him for allowing my older brother Vick to die alone in the bathroom. He had always been verbally and psychologically abusive to Vick by comparing him to me. For the most part, or so it seemed to him, I had my life together while Vick's was a mess.

About two years before Vick died, he had one of his legs amputated because he was diabetic and hadn't been taking care of himself. Nothing slows you down like losing a leg. I always told Vick that losing his leg was a blessing in disguise because it forced him to stop running the streets and focus on God before death came. In my eyes, he had plenty of time alone to reflect on his life, live the remainder for God's glory and wait for physical death to come so that he wouldn't feel pain anymore and go out with peace knowing that he would be with God for eternity. Vick didn't see it that way and was severely depressed. He would sit and soak in the tub for hours.

I had flown Vick out to spend his last Christmas with me in Maryland and begged him to stay since I had plenty of room in my home and my wife, TeErra, was cool with it because we were financially stable enough to easily support him. He declined my offer because he was in a rush to get back home to Milwaukee and his so-called friends.

I often referred to him as being in the Prodigal Son stage of spending time with fake friends and wasting his life away doing what he wanted to do. Unfortunately, he never made it out of the eating slop stage of that story while his family was living good. I can vividly recall begging him to stay in Maryland. When he refused, I hugged him when I dropped him off at the airport knowing it would be the last time I saw him. He died alone in the bathroom of heartbreak in our Milwaukee home with my pops on February of 2015 because he had stopped taking his medicine. I wasn't there so I'm not sure if he went out in peace or fear. I delivered his eulogy at the funeral.

When it came time for my pops to have someone take care of him in his last years, I thought it would be fitting and karmic for him to also die alone in the same home in Milwaukee. However, my mom helped me to see the bitterness in my heart and forgive him. We ended up moving him down to Atlanta where he stayed in a group home that would administer his medicines and make sure he made it to his doctor's appointment. Ironically, until the bitter end, he despised my mom and talked bad to her even though I constantly reminded him that he wouldn't be down in Atlanta without her. I am now glad that my kids got to spend time with their "PaPa" before he died and that I was able to forgive him and have real conversations with him. As I've said before, my mom has really shown me an example of agape love, because if I was in her position I couldn't have done the things she did for Pops.

In the last year of his life, my pops was able to live a good life, spending the weekends and sometimes weekdays at my or my sister's home eating "hell off the cross" and watching Netflix without disturbance. He was there to experience Christmas, Thanksgiving, birthdays and other awesome family moments surrounded by family and love. I'm so glad that God gave me time to forgive and move on from those feelings toward my father and older brother. The best way to forgive and love others is to look at what you've done to God and how many times He has forgiven you; it helps you to understand why you should also forgive. Remember to always thank God for His grace and mercy and forgive others the way you expect God to forgive you when you fail.

*

God provided me with everything I needed in spite of myself and there was nothing further that Mr.GoodGame would add to my life but trouble. I stopped chasing the world and finally realized the meaning of the scripture that had bugged me all my life: *Then said Jesus unto his disciples, If any man will come after me, let him deny himself, and take up his cross, and follow me. For whosoever will save his life shall lose it: and whosoever will lose his life for my sake shall find it. For what is a man profited, if he shall gain the whole world, and lose his own soul? or what shall a man give in exchange for his soul?* (Matthew 16:24-26)

I had to kill Mr.GoodGame to live fully and walk in my purpose.

EPILOGUE

Who I am today is far from who I was in this book. I am an active member of Renaissance Church of Christ located in Atlanta, Georgia, and I help lead its young adult ministry. I'm married to my lovely wife, TeErra Bingham, who is a stay-at-home mom caring for and homeschooling our eight-year-old Charlie Bingham III and three-year-old Carlie Bingham. I'm a successful entrepreneur who started a family-owned children's book company, and I'm a successful lawyer for a leading technology company. I've won several awards in my career for my legal work and my work in the diversity and inclusion space. I'm proud to be in a position personally and professionally to help make this a better, more inclusive world.

I used to be that guy unsure of my purpose, but I am now living in my purpose. I say that not to brag but to give glory to God because I never would've made it without Him. I've always tried to acknowledge Him so that He would direct my path, and He has done just that!

My mom instilled in me to remember who I am and whose I am, and these principles helped me not to give up in some of my darkest hours.

Fear can paralyze you and my fear of how people would judge me if they knew my past stopped me from sharing this full testimony. Clearly, there are some grotesque details about me and others in this book, but remember that none of this is fiction or exaggerated. Looking back at this period in my life provided me three very valuable insights. First, when I think about how merciful God has been to me, sharing intimate details about my life that most would keep secret is my reasonable service; especially if my mistakes, weaknesses and shame will help others turn and glorify God. As we grow spiritually and better recognize the mercies of God, being vulnerable and suffering for Christ's sake will be okay with us. Second, after you start to appreciate all His many blessings, with His mercies being just one of them, whatever you have to deal with following the guidance of the Holy Spirit, good or bad, you begin to trust and understand is well worth it and your reasonable service. Finally, when you recognize and start to walk in your purpose, you tend to get better at recognizing when Satan enters the mix to distract you from your purpose.

God preserved me through my struggles despite my shortcomings and I hope that sharing this journey with you will help you to see or remember that God loves you, you are fearfully and wonderfully made, and God can use you for His purposes despite your many flaws. You can use your talents for good or for evil. If God could use a savage like me, He can definitely use you.

Spread God's love, speak the truth without fear, walk by faith and acknowledge Him in all your ways.

ABOUT THE AUTHOR

Born and raised in Milwaukee, success for people like Charlie Bingham Jr. was bound to be short-lived and ill-begotten. With the confidence of a king and the backing of the Kingdom, Charlie outmaneuvered the odds. Earning his Juris Doctorate at the Howard University School of Law, Charlie is an accomplished tech attorney who returns to Howard annually to recruit students.

An optimistic doer, Charlie improves the world by capitalizing on God-given strengths and encouraging others. Whether using his testimony to help others restore their faith or raising awareness about diversity in the legal profession, he passionately uses what he's learned to help others.

Also passionate about African-American culture, entrepreneurship, and generating wealth,

Charlie started a children's book publishing company, which features lessons his children have learned. Residing in Atlanta, Charlie enjoys mentoring, basketball, video games, traveling, and spending time with his family.

Learn more at
www.thedeathofmrgoodgame.com

CREATING DISTINCTIVE BOOKS WITH INTENTIONAL RESULTS

We're a collaborative group of creative masterminds with a mission to produce high-quality books to position you for monumental success in the marketplace.

Our professional team of writers, editors, designers, and marketing strategists work closely together to ensure that every detail of your book is a clear representation of the message in your writing.

Want to know more?
Write to us at info@publishyourgift.com
or call (888) 949-6228

Discover great books, exclusive offers, and more at
www.PublishYourGift.com

Connect with us on social media

@publishyourgift

Milton Keynes UK
Ingram Content Group UK Ltd.
UKHW022257190124
436352UK00005B/134